"I have had Michele Perr[y] ... Supernatural Ministry an[d] ... Baker; when we have talked about Michele, we say, 'She is the real thing.' I consider Michele and her missionary work among the top two works I am aware of, second only to Rolland and Heidi Baker. She truly lives a supernatural life with supernatural courage, faith, provision, healings and miracles. Her stories are truly awesome; her story is even more awesome. Her new book, *An Invitation to the Supernatural Life*, is a must read."

Randy Clark, overseer of the Apostolic Network of Global Awakening; co-author with Bill Johnson of *The Essential Guide to Healing* and *Healing Unplugged*; author of *There Is More*

"Many write books on the supernatural after reading other books on the supernatural. Michele is different. She teaches from firsthand experience how to live a supernatural life naturally. Her book is a major mentoring tool for your life."

Sid Roth, host of the *It's Supernatural!* television show

"Enjoy the adventure of a lifetime as Michele Perry explores the possibilities of life in the supernatural realm. Live Michele's real-life experiences as she shares how heaven touches earth through God's faithful servants. Michele descriptively invigorates readers as they quickly discover secrets of God's heart shared by one's supernatural faith experiences. *An Invitation to the Supernatural Life* is a must-read adventure into the supernatural for all believers."

Bob Jones, Bob Jones Ministries

"Michele is one of the extraordinary missionaries in these times, and this book could elevate her status as a serious teacher and apologist for sound, biblical Christianity, which the supernatural life is. Very well done, Michele."

Rick Joyner, executive director
of MorningStar Ministries

"In *An Invitation to the Supernatural Life*, Michele Perry offers readers a powerful glimpse into the unseen spiritual realm. Her faith is contagious and will draw you into the possibility of experiencing this realm in your own life."

Francis and Judith MacNutt, co-founders
of Christian Healing Ministries, Inc.; authors
of *Healing* and *Angels Are for Real*

AN
INVITATION
TO THE
SUPERNATURAL
LIFE

AN
INVITATION

TO THE

SUPERNATURAL
LIFE

MICHELE PERRY

Chosen

a division of Baker Publishing Group
Minneapolis, Minnesota

© 2012 by Michele Perry

Published by Chosen Books
11400 Hampshire Avenue South
Bloomington, Minnesota 55438
www.chosenbooks.com

Chosen Books is a division of
Baker Publishing Group, Grand Rapids, Michigan

Printed in the United States of America

Library of Congress Cataloging-in-Publication Data
Perry, Michele, 1977–
    An invitation to the supernatural life / Michele Perry.
      p. cm.
    ISBN 978-0-8007-9533-7 (pbk. : alk. paper)
    1. Christian life. 2. Spiritual life—Christianity. 3. Supernatural. I. Title.
BV4501.3.P47 2012
248.4—dc23   2012002136

The internet addresses, email addresses, and phone numbers in this book are accurate at the time of publication. They are provided as a resource. Baker Publishing Group does not endorse them or vouch for their content or permanence.

Cover design by Dan Pitts

12   13   14   15   16   17   18   7   6   5   4   3   2   1

green press INITIATIVE

To all those who dare to embrace the unpaved road into
His heart and live out a yes-cry with their lives.

Contents

Foreword

I'm impressed. *An Invitation to the Supernatural Life* by Michele Perry is amazing. Not that I would have expected anything less. I wouldn't. Most anyone who knows her would say she should be the poster child for supernatural courage. I am just pleasantly surprised at *how* good this book is. It really is amazing.

Michele could move any of us to tears simply by telling her story. She personifies devotion, resolve and courage. And while there are wonderful bits of her experience sprinkled throughout the book, keeping it authentic, she uses her brilliant insights and an inspirational writing style to move readers to places they might not have expected to go.

To merge the practical with the mystical takes an unusual gift. Michele has done just that—wonderfully. In fact, she presents the life that we all hunger for but cannot obtain outside of becoming childlike. This book, in a sense, is true wisdom.

Her life is one of absolute surrender. Adversity, mixed with God encounters, helped this dear one to settle in her quest to know Jesus at a very young age. Her honesty about her own adversities and other disqualifying factors are very disarming. In fact, I found it hard to read of such a journey without looking for the opportunity to display similar faith and courage for myself. She removes all the reasons that anyone would have for not being qualified for a supernatural lifestyle. She overcame, against all odds. And now I must.

While I believe this book would help many seasoned ministers of the Gospel around the world, I hope it finds its way into the hands of the everyday believer—the ones who think their lot in life is simply to support those who do the important stuff. My prayer is that *An Invitation to the Supernatural Life* would be used as a lightning rod, attracting the activities of heaven into the lives of unsuspecting servants of the Lord, who never thought it within their grasp to live as Jesus did. It is. And we must!

Michele states in her introduction: "When I read someone's revelation of Him [Jesus], it can become a doorway of faith that unlocks more of my own. But one thing I have yet to find is a book that shares practical keys to embracing a life filled with personal encounters, a book that helps you learn how to see and experience the realms of heaven you are created for. You might call this my attempt to bridge the gap." Congratulations, Michele Perry! You have succeeded. And we are all better for it.

Bill Johnson
Senior Pastor of Bethel Church, Redding, California
Author of *When Heaven Invades Earth*
and co-author of *The Essential Guide to Healing*

Acknowledgments

Thank you to all of those who have stood with me believing for this book to become reality amidst the storms and joys of the birth of this new nation of South Sudan.

Thank you to my family here in South Sudan: My children and our staff, both Sudanese and missionary, you all are my heroes, and I learn so much from you every day.

Thank you to my friends and family around the world who have challenged me to stretch further, dive deeper and fly higher. You are the ones who have cheered me on to new levels of faith and grace.

To Heidi and Rolland, Mel, Karen L., Becky and Byron, Mary-Pat and Bill, Briskilla, Ian, Justin and Rachel, Karen D., Luci and Amelia: Thank you for being there and for being inspiration, creative sounding boards and those who have surrounded me with your love and prayers.

To those who have made this book a reality: Jane, your literary insight and encouragements have again helped make this book into what it now is. I have learned so much from you again—thank you. My family with Chosen, it has once again been an honor and privilege to travel more miles and new chapters together.

And most of all I want to thank my beautiful Jesus, who walked into my room so many years ago and started me on the journey found within these pages.

Introduction

The Language of Invitation

Sweet friend,

I am so glad you are here. Yes, YOU who are reading these lines and loops right now. Welcome!

I hope and pray our journeys together through the following pages will become an invitation into the amazing supernatural destiny in Jesus you have been created for.

I have read many books on intimacy with Jesus, and living with Him by faith. I savor the testimonies of people who have seen heaven and had profound revelations from Him that have changed their lives. They line my bookshelves.

I am always hungry for more. I am encouraged by every supernatural encounter I read or hear of because I know the testimony of Jesus is the spirit of prophecy (Revelation 19:10). When I read someone's revelation from Him, it can become a doorway of faith that unlocks more of my own.

But one thing I have yet to find is a book that shares practical keys to embracing a life filled with your own personal encounters, a book that helps you learn how to see and experience the realms of heaven you are created for. You might call this my attempt to help bridge that gap. May there be many more books that join it.

Walking in God's supernatural kingdom was never supposed to be a complicated exercise only available to the spiritually elite. Meeting Him, seeing Him, knowing Him, interacting with the unseen realms we are created for should be the most natural, simple, accessible reality in our lives. It isn't just for missionaries living in Africa or those who minister publicly on a stage; it is for all of us. It is for you who are reading these words right now.

But before we go any further, I have a confession to make. I still don't get all my terms right. There is so much terminology surrounding ways of meeting God, ways of receiving from Him, and everyone seems to use their terms a little differently, if they even use them at all.

For our purposes, I use the term *encounter* generally to refer to those times when Jesus reveals Himself to us very directly, where we *encounter* Him in the realm of His kingdom or He encounters us in the realm of earth. There are many ways He comes, many ways He speaks, and many ways He reveals Himself to us in those times. We'll be talking more about those as we journey onward.

I will warn you, however. I am not writing an academic discussion about biblical mysticism or supernatural realities. Academic discussions so often stop at "about." About can be so impersonal, so clinical. This is an invitation to enter into God's fullness for yourself.

I am very simple. I see life in metaphor and analogy. I meet Jesus in small, grimy fingers weaving their way into mine and in little eyes that twinkle and laugh.

I meet Him in butterfly chases, predawn blankets of silence and diamond-studded canopies at night that steal my breath away. I meet Him in the everyday grace of ordinary life as much as I do in revelatory encounters and miracles. Neither to me is more holy than the other. All the ways He comes are utterly supernatural. I want everything He desires to give because the full reality of the supernatural realm of His kingdom is truly as close to us as the air we breathe.

It is my heart to weave the ways of encountering and releasing His supernatural kingdom together for you, dear reader, in such a way you might understand how profoundly they are woven together for me. Making grubby hugs holy and tangibly walking with Jesus normal.

If you already have your terms down, please forgive my simplicity when I use them sparingly or a bit creatively. If you perchance are desiring academic explanations about revelatory or prophetic giftings or hearing God's voice, you will be pleased to know there are many, many books out there that can explain it all far better than I. If you find any of this a foreign language, I do promise to define my terminology as I introduce it. And, if you are reading this hungry, I humbly offer the grace of a shared journey into the more of Jesus you were created for.

From the unpaved road,
Michele Perry
Yei, South Sudan

1

Invited In

The muted sounds of my father's television drift through the wall and settle in the air around me. I am sitting on the floor in my childhood bedroom in northeast Florida. Olive green almost-shag carpet pushes its way between my toes like grass trying to grow. You know that 1970s olive green that came with mustard yellow and a color called rust? Yes, *that* green. I close my eyes and lift my face to the liquid warmth streaming through my window. "Sunlight must be what God's love feels like," I ponder quietly.

Curled up in a pool of sunshine, sitting on worn green carpet reminiscent of decades gone by, I wait.

Five minutes pass. Ten minutes.

"What are you waiting for?" you may ask.

I am waiting to hear what God sounds like. But I do not know how to tell you that at fifteen years old because I am not yet sure myself.

As I wait, my mind flashes back to several days before, when this whole story started.

The God Who Still Speaks

Books are my best friends. They are safe and somewhat predictable, adventurous and mysterious all at the same time. A good book can transport you clear across the world in the blink of an eye. If your world needs transporting, as mine sometimes does, books are very good friends to have. But for all my travels through their pages, part of my heart still cannot escape the desperate desire for something more.

Today, just one day before the school days will spill us out into summer, I step across the threshold of our local used bookshop, watching dust particles stirred by my presence dance around me in the afternoon light.

An old wire mesh bin near the door, slightly bent and rusted, is stacked high with discarded words waiting to be sold for pennies on the page. I never know whether I will find mystery, adventure, wisdom or poetry hidden in its depths.

Rummaging through the dusty selections, I am unimpressed with what I see. Promises of intrigue and drama, faraway places and undiscovered tales all fall somehow flat, like a note fighting to reach its place on the staff. For several weeks, there has been a gnawing unsettledness deepening in my heart. I am soon to know it as a gift called hunger. But for the moment, I just feel agitated and itchy, empty on the inside.

Some of heaven's greatest invitations begin with hunger.

I turn away in disappointment, studying the dust bunnies holding conventions in the corners around me. No new

20

friends today. But something inside of me turns my gaze back for one final glance before leaving empty-handed.

There it is. How did I miss it? Sitting at the back of the bin, half-covered over by other choices, is a fat paperback, its title barely visible. *Something More.* Somehow these two words call forth the unspoken stirrings in my soul. I rescue it from the recesses of the bargain pile. Anticipation lets loose fluttering butterfly wings against the wall of my chest as I scan its back cover. I know I have what I came for.

Written by an author I have never heard of, Catherine Marshall, this book looks as if it was written before I was born. I love that about writing. Black and white lines and loops filling blank canvases defy time itself. I love that about this book. It has hope of surviving me and reaching out to a day that is not yet. Maybe one spring afternoon it will be this book's turn, the one you are reading now, to be rescued from the obscurity of a bargain bin. But I am getting ahead of myself.

For several days, *Something More* sits quietly on my dresser. Its slightly yellowed, dog-eared pages watch me come and go. It waits patiently, ready to wrap me in the words of another's journey.

It is the story of one woman's walk through love and loss, to be embraced by grace.

Chapters melt away before me until one small paragraph arrests my attention. It is almost an aside, an oh-by-the-way. I am so grateful for the asides of life. The author mentions ever so briefly her writing down in a notebook what she senses God speaking to her.

Even the syllables of those few lines explode, ricocheting through my spirit. Could it be? Can it be true that God is still speaking now? I flip to the front page to see when the book was published.

Wow, God, I thought. *She was alive in the 1970s. We are in the 1990s. That was only twenty years ago. You must still be speaking. And, if You would speak to her, surely You'd want to talk to me too!*

I grab a blue ballpoint pen and an old spiral notebook half-filled with last week's biology notes. I am determined, impetuous even. Resolutely, I plant myself on that olive green carpet and say, "Jesus, I want to hear Your voice. And I am not moving until I do."

And so my daily journey with the God who still speaks begins.

Was That Me or Was That God?

This resolute declaration of my heart starts me on a trail of learning about how God speaks. Sometimes He speaks with words. Then there are times He communicates in ways that seem to utterly defy them. The adventure comes in learning how to receive all that He is saying in all the ways He says it.

So here I am sitting on my bedroom floor listening to the muffled sounds of a fight scene echoing from my father's TV across the hall. I meant what I said. I am determined not to move until I know what He sounds like. Armed with pen and paper, I am ready to record whatever He might choose to share.

I wait.

It seemed to work for Catherine Marshall, so why not Michele Perry?

I wait five minutes, ten minutes. I hear nothing but periodic silence punctuated with sound effects from a high-speed chase through the door. Questions begin to swirl whirlpools in my mind. I fight not to be sucked into them.

What does God sound like? Will He speak through a big booming loudspeaker from the sky? How will I know if it is Him?

"Um, helloooooooo God. I'm waiting here."

Have you ever felt like that? Waiting to hear from Him, but not even sure what it is exactly you are waiting for?

Fifteen minutes pass, and then twenty. My dad turns off his TV to go and do yard work. I am left alone with the silence and my questions. Both are deafening.

"Hi, um, God. Yes, hi there. It's me. I am still here. I even have my notebook ready. See?"

Twenty-five minutes, then thirty minutes pass. I know because I watch them tick by, falling from the present into the past. The clock on my night table chronicles their relentless descent. I start to feel very silly, and my mental to-do list begins to push its way into my thoughts. Homework assignments, project deadlines, chores still undone—all dance with the uncertainty of my waiting.

Have you ever had that nagging sense that you could be so much more productive than sitting around positioning yourself for a revelation you are not sure will ever come?

I resist the urge to be productive elsewhere. I have the sense that I am on the edge of something. It is only His grace that keeps me still, keeps me in the waiting.

"Jesus, I meant it. I am not moving until I hear You. Just so You know."

He really loves impetuous, hungry fifteen-year-olds waiting for Him on green almost-shag carpet that should have stayed in the seventies.

Suddenly, quietly, distinctively, a thought comes so clearly into my heart it was as if I had "heard" it from outside of myself. Indeed, I had.

"Don't worry, beloved, you will hear Me."

A whisper no louder than the sunshine puddled on the floor around me, but it shoots like lightning through my soul. Surprised, I literally jump. Everything inside me leaps up from my stomach to my throat in expectation. Was that Him? Was that me? Did I just make that up? I wonder.

Was that me or was that God?

Have you ever asked that question? If you have, you are not alone.

Another thought passes through my mind. I am quite sure I did not come up with it. It occurs to me that the Holy Spirit might speak in thoughts we would never think ourselves.

"Jesus, if this is really You, could You give me a Bible verse or something to confirm that this is really You, and I am not making all this up?"

Immediately, and I do mean immediately, a verse reference flashes into my mind's eye, reminding me of the insistence of flashing announcement signs on the highway. It is that clear.

"John 6:20. John 6:20. John 6:20."

I scramble to find a Bible, which I have read only very selectively at this point. A psalm or two, a passage of Jesus talking in the gospels with the red letters, a few stories from Acts . . . I do not know where much is even beyond Psalm 23. Thank heavens for the table of contents!

Eagerly, I search out the passage and flip the Bible open to John 6:20.

There it is in bold red print, the one line that forever changes my life: "It is I—do not be afraid."

24

"Oh my gosh, Jesus, I can hear You! I can hear God! It really is You!"

My life will never be the same.

His Invitation

That one encounter with His still, small voice at age fifteen became for me an invitation to listen and lean into Him, to get to know Him more every day until my listening and my knowing became as effortless as my breathing.

Knowing you can hear God's voice is just an entry point into a supernatural love adventure with Jesus that will never end.

Just so you know, in case you were wondering: I have not arrived. As if you thought I had!

But every day I am learning more of Him. Some days all I can do is stand in grace and genuinely wonder how I have gotten to where I am. But always the more of who He is calls me to leave behind the safe confines of my known moments to enter into the eternity found in His heart.

I would love to share some of this journey with you, dear reader. Shared journeys are gifts of grace in a too often solitary world.

You, too, can know Jesus deeply, intimately, profoundly. It is what you were created for. He is waiting to show Himself to you in ways more precious than you can imagine. There is something more, and that something more is Him.

Finding Stillness

After a few years of practice in hearing the ways God speaks with words, in my late teens I started a whole new chapter of my journey learning to hear Him in places beyond them. Enter a field of cows in Texas and one very surprised city girl.

The yellow-green grass of an early spring dripped with liquid silence that Saturday morning. Gentle light peered over the horizon watching a new day begin. I quietly got up from my mattress on the cabin floor, so as not to disturb the sleeping women around me. I still was not sure why I was there. Except someone had invited me. Invitations are powerful things.

Silence. Our culture teaches us it is the enemy. iPods set on endless repeat, TVs providing ambient noise, sound filling our hours and days with auditory clutter. Why is that? Why do I embrace this need for noise? Is there a place in my heart that is running from itself? I wondered all these things as I woke to my first morning of silence, my first day on a silent retreat with thirty other women wondering roughly the same things.

The night before we were issued a challenge: to meet with God beyond the place of words for at least the first half of the next day. Could we so deeply enter His presence that even the veil of language itself would fall off our hearts? Could we let the Word in flesh simply be, to dwell among us?

All the God-meetings I had known till then were wrapped up in speech. Words had been my friends since I discovered them. They defined my world; stacks of journals were my legacy. I was in the university studying right then to get a degree in their usage.

To meet with God in a place beyond words . . . was this possible? To meet Him in silence . . . would we even recognize one another, stripped of syllables and discourse?

I didn't know, but I wanted to find out. I silently put on coat and shoe, slipping out the cabin door into the morning mist. A large piece of land far out in the country called me to explore its edges: a place filled with trails and streams and wide-open places where creation still praises her Creator. For a city girl, such quietness was a foreign land. I wandered my way down trails and across brooks until I reached a meadow.

Sunlight dripped off the grass around me, danced through the trees until it landed at my feet. The silence enveloped my yesterday and tomorrow, leaving behind only now. Now was the moment I had to meet with Him. I came bare in that moment, stripped even of language into His presence.

I could handle not talking—but not writing, not journaling, not even thinking in words at all? What would be left to meet Him with?

I sat down in the sunlight, not unlike a few years before, except this time I had literal grass pushing its way between my toes. And again I waited: my breath, my only audible prayer. I closed my eyes and allowed the stillness around me to fill the noise within.

Slowly, gradually, I became aware of His familiar presence. The Holy Spirit blew in like a faint, barely-there breeze. He really was with me. Stripped by the silence, I found myself not the star student, not the aspiring missionary, not the prodigious child, but me—the dearly loved daughter of her Father in heaven. Just me.

Stripped by the silence, I found Him. Not as I had ever met Him before, but in His weighty I AM presence. Together we just were. And that was enough.

While I sat in stillness, a picture of Jesus sitting with me began to be painted in my mind.

These pictures painted on the screen of our thoughts by Him are called visions. When we allow God to meet with us beyond words, many times He speaks in images and pictures, or visions. We are created to see into the unseen. Visual encounters with God fill the pages of Scripture and are our inheritance as His dearly loved children. We'll talk about visions in much greater detail in Chapter 3.

It was very faint at first, this vision of mine, like looking through a thick early morning fog, when people appear as mere forms and shadows of what they are. Yet in the haze is enshrouded the real. When you get close enough to see, the more you look, the closer you get, the form finds a face and a voice as it walks past. Starting to see things in the kingdom, the realm of God's Spirit, can be very similar at times.

In this vision Jesus lifted my face till His eyes met mine with oceans of liquid love. You could get lost in those eyes. He then picked me up and spun me around, setting me down in another field. Suddenly, I saw it clearly. It was a field called grace. It was a movie being played across my thoughts. But it was somehow more than even that.

Jesus leaned down, scooped up a bouquet of wildflowers from around us. I reached out to take them, and they all turned to butterflies that danced freedom into my heart. He took one look at my face and laughed the most beautiful laugh I had ever heard. It was rich like honey. It was like the sound of mountain streams rushing over rocks accented by a bird's song. He looked deep into my eyes and said, "In you I am well pleased."

The life those words contained sank into the deep places where I had often wondered if I would ever be pleasing enough. Silence delivered truth to my soul.

As quickly as this vision came, it faded, leaving me back in a grassy field in the rolling hills of east Texas. I experienced peace just being with Him. I lay in the grass breathing it all in. The grass rustled soft around me. Then a bell rang faintly in the distance, signaling breakfast, and I reluctantly pried open my eyes.

With a sharp intake of breath, I clamped my hand hard over my mouth, barely preventing a startled scream from escaping my lips. I was nose to nose with a large white dairy cow with haphazard black spots. Her melted chocolate eyes framed with lash-like forests looked curiously into mine. I sat up carefully, my heart racing, only to realize I was surrounded by dairy cows grazing around me!

Somehow I must have wandered off the land into a nearby pasture. Putting a city girl in the country could be a dangerous thing!

Shock gave way to nervous giggles that refused to stay put in my belly. I wondered if this broke the rules of the *silent* retreat. Probably. I was no longer being silent. But only the cows heard, and they didn't seem to mind.

I must confess: this was my first time to meet a cow up close and personal. Someone once told me that in the presence of large animals you should move very slowly. So I did. Very carefully, in slow motion, I extracted myself from their breakfast time to go have my own.

In the middle of a cow field in Texas I discovered that one of His greatest gifts to me is the invitation to let Him speak through stillness in a place that defies the very words I had defined my world by.

We Owe the World an Encounter

Years and miles have passed between the times I first learned about hearing God speak both with words and then beyond them as a teenager and when I came to my current home in South Sudan in 2006.

I arrived here with little more than the promises of Jesus. Most people told me along the way I was insane. "You crazy white woman" was the common sentiment. Some days I wondered if they were right.

I mean, I don't look like a very likely candidate. I am a one-legged, artistically inclined city girl whose idea of a survival kit still includes mascara. Bugs, dirt and I don't get along at all. I told Jesus the two things I really didn't do were camping and children. Heaven laughed.

It has not been easy. But journeys worth taking rarely are. For those of you I have not met yet, I live in the bush of South Sudan and have more than one hundred children calling me mama. On one hand, it is a very normal life of soccer games, PTA meetings, snotty noses and dirty feet. On the other, it is a daily invitation to encounter heaven in the places of my deepest need and weakness.

Truly, it is not what I expected my life to look like. But that is part of the adventure of knowing Him. Following His heart can lead you down some unexpected, even unpaved roads— days filled with grubby hugs, precious smiles, no running water or electricity and overwhelming need seem a strange place to discover what I am created for. This is especially true since my idea of camping is still a day spa.

I want to tell you more about living and serving in the bush of South Sudan. I will do so as we journey together through the rest of this book. But first let me share with you what I once heard Bill Johnson say: "We owe the world an encounter with God."

That statement has provoked a question that still echoes

in the depth of my heart: What does it mean to become His love encounter in the earth? Dear reader, what does that look like in your world?

It is a compelling question. And it is one I don't have any profound answers, sure-fire formulas or seven-step models to give you in response.

But one thing has become blatantly obvious to me. I cannot give away to anyone something I do not have myself. I cannot impart what is not a part of me. If I am going to bring people into a real encounter with who Jesus is, I need to be living in an ongoing, deepening relationship with Him every day.

And that is basically what this book is about. My ultimate purpose in writing goes beyond sharing my own story with you. I don't want you to just read of someone else's story; I want you, dear reader, to live out your own.

Call it the oxygen mask principle. I spend roughly a third of my life on airplanes flying around to different places to share lessons I am learning on this unpaved road called my life. Every flight starts out with nearly the same introduction, which is why I virtually have it memorized. If you are a fellow frequent flier, you probably already know it well.

"Put your tray tables and seat backs in their full upright and locked positions in preparation for takeoff. Please make sure your seat belts are fastened low and tight across your lap. This cabin is pressurized for your comfort. In the unlikely event that the cabin pressure should change, oxygen masks will drop from a compartment above your head. Please pull the mask toward you and place it over your nose and mouth. Oxygen will be flowing even though the bag does not inflate. If you are traveling with or seated next to someone needing assistance, *put your own mask on first and then offer assistance.*"

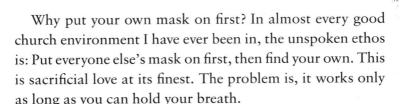

Why put your own mask on first? In almost every good church environment I have ever been in, the unspoken ethos is: Put everyone else's mask on first, then find your own. This is sacrificial love at its finest. The problem is, it works only as long as you can hold your breath.

Why put your own mask on first? Because you cannot help your neighbor breathe the life-giving atmosphere of another realm if you are unconscious from not breathing it yourself. You cannot give what you do not have. This book is a call to make sure your own oxygen mask is in place so you have something to give.

For the last two decades, I have been on a quest to live a life of intimate friendship with Jesus. It is my prayer that in these pages you will find practical keys to unlock your own deepening understanding of who He is.

Every story, every insight, every word is about embracing His invitation to enter into supernatural reality you were created for. Anything you read in these pages you can have. It is *for you*.

Can you hear the call to discover more of God, where the deepest longings in your heart will be met by the depths of His? Dare with me to risk an intimacy that will unleash your destiny. Say yes to a journey of practically learning to know His voice and walk in the unseen realms of His kingdom.

Are you up for the adventure? Are you ready to step into the raw, untamed wildness of His love and the audacity of His dreams? Are you willing to leave behind a known path for lesser-taken hidden trails into the deep places of His Spirit? Are you hungry to know Jesus more even if it costs you what once was dear to you? Have you ever wanted to know His voice more clearly and understand how practically to live a life that brings "on earth as it is in heaven" to pass? Do you long to see God move in power in and through your life in the ways you have heard He moves in faraway places like Africa?

If so, I am writing this book for you.

You are created for encounter. It is for *you*. You are created to live in a reality far greater than what your natural eyes see. All throughout Scripture are stories of God showing Himself to His people in visions and dreams, in wonders of His incredible kindness. Even Jesus said that we would do greater things than He did. I for one really want to walk out what that looks like!

You sitting there with these pages in your hands are not reading this book by accident. It is a divine appointment with destiny.

After all, if you know Him, you really do owe the world around you an encounter with who He is.

Invitation to Enter In

I said in the introduction that this book is all about invitation. You, dear, amazing reader, are invited in. You are not asked to stand on the outside observing someone else's revelation. You are called into experiencing your own.

Come. Enter into stillness, into His presence, into a walk that straddles heaven and earth.

"Beloved," Jesus once whispered to me, before the stars had even left the sky, "My original intention is your ultimate invitation."

Sometimes Jesus speaks in mysteries and riddles to call me on a mission of exploration. The point isn't just the meaning; it is the time I spend with Him to discover it. I know that.

His statement, then, gave rise to questions that rolled around in my thoughts as I watched the sun chase the stars to sleep.

What was God's original intention in creating the world? In creating me? And how did it become my invitation? What was I being invited into?

Understanding that riddle took me back to the very beginning of it all. Did God create the world just to have something to rule, to have more ministries and a lot of people serving Him obediently?

I think there is something far deeper, way bigger that God wants to bring us into. I believe Father, Son and Holy Spirit have such an extravagant love relationship among themselves that they simply want to share their love with an ever-growing family of sons and daughters.

This book is about how to know Jesus more through receiving revelation from Him. But our invitation to live in encounter with Jesus every day is far more than an invitation to a series of experiences alone.

We must have experiences. I do not slight them in the least. Truth is biblically known only when it has become part of our experiential life. But an experience without the right context to put it in risks being misunderstood, wrongly applied.

At the core of who God is: He is love (see 1 John 4:16). And this God kind of love is impossible outside of relationship. Father, Son and Holy Spirit have all the relational fulfillment they will ever need within themselves. But their love is so big, so good, so compelling that they are not content to keep it to themselves.

God created the world not out of need, but out of love. Which means that you and I were created not out of need, but out of love and for love. You are created, fashioned for,

34

called into the same love relationship with God that He enjoys within Himself. And you are called to become a reflection of Him in which the fullness of His love can rest in the earth.

This is the ultimate invitation and context for a daily walk of encounter. Father, Son, Holy Spirit sharing themselves with you and transforming you to look like them. It is what you were created for. When you truly get hold of that in your heart, it will change *every*thing. And it is this reality that makes the rest of your journey possible.

Practical Keys: How to Make a Still Space

Dear reader, in the pages of this book, I want to share practical insight and offer regular opportunities for you to stop reading and start experiencing. These are little things that have helped me in my own walk, and I hope might be helpful for you, too. I offer them not as rules to follow but as possibilities for you to explore.

One of the most important keys I have found in going deeper with Jesus is to make space every day for stillness. As mama to over one hundred children and a leader of a growing ministry, I know that is not an easy feat.

For most of us from the West, stillness is completely countercultural. Our days are set by alarms and agendas, filled with messaging and email, texting and technology. My U.S. cell phone can even ring in the bush in Sudan! Have you ever noticed how easy it is to become fully accessible to everyone everywhere and fully present to no one at all? How much more so with God.

If we want a lifestyle of encountering Jesus, we need to make space for that to happen.

For most of us, stillness will never find us. I have learned I must go in pursuit of it. Silence is a humbling thing. It pulls out from under me all the things with which I prop up even my relationship with God. But when I allow it to do its work, it becomes a foundational platform for encounter.

How do we pursue stillness? Jesus has great things to say about finding the secret places of meeting with Him. He often withdrew and went to the lonely places to be with Father God (see Luke 5:16).

> "But you, when you pray, go into your inner room, close your door and pray to your Father who is in secret, and your Father who sees what is done in secret will reward you."
>
> Matthew 6:6, NASB

Jesus was talking about making space for encounter. Most Jewish homes back in the day did not have inner rooms or even doors. So what on earth did He mean?

Perhaps it was a call to find the secret, solitary places to meet with God. Or, if they could not be found, to create them wherever it was possible.

Or perhaps He was not speaking of a physical place at all.

> "Nor will they say, 'See here!' or 'See there!' For indeed, the kingdom of God is within you."
>
> Luke 17:21

If the kingdom of God is within me, then I always have access to it by faith. It is closer to me than the air I breathe.

Wherever on earth I travel, including right here in South Sudan, I have come to know the inner room as the interior

36

place inside my life where His kingdom lives. I enter it simply by faith and shut the door on outside distraction. And there I draw into a still place where I become aware of His presence and can enter into all He has for the moment.

After some years of practice, I can enter this place in my spirit anywhere at any time. But even so, having a still space around me in the natural, physical realm has been crucial in my learning how to embrace stillness and find this interior meeting place with God.

Creating a still space might mean muting the cell phone for an hour and letting voice mail intervene. It might be turning off the TV. It might include not making email and Facebook the first priority of the morning. Or even the second. Yes, I am preaching to myself mostly here on this last one!

No matter what our circumstances are, we can make space in our lives for time that is His alone if it is priority enough. It is all about finding the rhythm of rest, the pace of grace.

May I share some suggestions that have helped me create space for stillness in my own life? Again, these are only suggestions.

- Put your cell phone on mute and out of sight when you are having time with God. Let voice mail do its duty. The texts will still be there when you are ready to respond to them.

- Turn your house phone off or go to a room that doesn't have a phone in it. Then you will not be so tempted to answer it. Turn on the answering machine and let it serve you.

- Turn off the television, except when you are actually watching it. You'd be surprised how much easier it is to hear God when you reduce the external background noise around you.

- Don't let email or social media define your time or set the pace for your day.

- Find a quiet place. If you are like me and quiet places are in short supply, find a time when everyone else is asleep or otherwise engaged.

- If you can dedicate a place to your alone time with God (even if it is just the same end of the sofa), sometimes a little routine and a familiar spot really help displace the noise.

- Consider finding time at the beginning of the day before your mind and spirit have begun to race.

- Sit comfortably with a favorite cup of coffee or tea, a journal, your Bible and just be. If you like fragranced candles, as I do, light one of your favorites. Breathe deeply. I have a cranberry candle, one that I hauled over thousands of miles to Africa, that is burning beside me right now.

- If the thousand-item to-do list starts forming in your mind, have a piece of paper accessible on which you can write down bullet points so you know you can return to them later. Once an item is written down, turn your focus back to Him.

- If you want to quiet your heart by listening to worship music, fabulous. But just make sure it leads you to a place of stillness when it's finished.

- Stop talking. Start listening and looking. God will speak and show you things. He really will.

May I pray for you?

Sweet Jesus, I ask that You would engulf my new friend read-ing this right now in Your tangible presence. Surround him, surround her with a blanket of Your stillness. Quiet all that shouts within until Your faintest whispers are heard more loudly than everything else.

I ask that You would show him or her creative ways to make space to encounter You every day. Wrap this dear reader up in Your love, Your arms bringing a hug all the way from heaven just for him, just for her. Open their ears and eyes to receive all that You desire to share. Awaken expectancy within for the more that each of us is created for!

Discussion Questions and Activation Exercise

In the rest of this book, we will explore more of what God is inviting us into in this supernatural life with Him. We will look at some of the myths that might hold us back, how to walk through the dry times and come out of desert places leaning on Him. We will look at ways to receive from Jesus and engage the fullness of His kingdom realm we are cre-ated for.

At the end of each chapter, I will include some discussion questions for personal journaling or sharing in a small group in case you'd like to invite some more friends to journey with us, as well as activation exercises to help you start your own walk in the realm of daily encounter with Jesus. Welcome to the first set of these!

- Describe a time when you heard God's voice. What did His voice sound like?

- Describe a time when you felt unsettled, hungry for more. Turn it into a prayer for God to stir the gift of hunger in your own soul for Him.
- What have you believed you were created for? Has it ever gotten in the way of simply enjoying Him?
- How does hearing you are created purely for the pleasure of God make you feel?
- How can you create more space for stillness in your life? What are some external and internal sources of noise you might need to turn off? Are you willing to do this? Ask Him to help you.
- What does God's ultimate invitation look like to you?

Activation: Take a weekday or weekend morning off alone with Jesus. Go someplace quiet, walk in the woods, sit by a stream, just spending time listening to Him beyond the place of words. And while you are there, try to avoid grazing cattle herds.

2

Seated in Heavenly Places

Kettle whistling wild, I rise to remove it from the fire. The blue gas flame from my weathered propane camp stove heats the kettle almost to the point of frenzy.

It is time for an evening cup of tea. I push my blue plastic chair back from my white plastic table-desk, slip arms into metal cuffs and step across the tile to enter my kitchen. It is a small block room just wide enough to turn around in. There a stainless steel kettle I hauled over half a continent from South Africa sings to me of its readiness to be poured out. I take my purple pansy fine china mug, fill it with steaming water and tea bag. Mindlessly, I jostle the string up and down, add sugar and powdered milk before sitting back at my plastic kitchen table-desk.

Warm soothing sips wrap around me from the inside out as I stare at this blank page and blinking cursor thinking of what to write to you.

Suddenly gunfire and celebratory squeals interrupt my train of thought. An all-out melee of joy can be heard from all over the compound. I abandon my tea and writing to see the celebration.

This is no ordinary night. Bullets fire red ribbons into the January 2011 night sky. There is a new nation yelling in celebration. The announcement has come. I step out of my small brick and mortar house and am literally swept off my feet with excited hugs from my children and family here.

"Mama, you helped us pray it in. Five years. You were here standing with us. Tonight it is official: We are a new nation. We are free. God has answered our prayers."

In 2005, the then warring south and north regions of Sudan signed a comprehensive peace agreement. According to its provisions, in 2011 South Sudan could vote whether to stay one with the north or separate and become independent. The vote was unanimous for independence.

I stand long with my family under the stars. I look up and see His diamond promises in the sky and then look down to see His manifested promise all around me. We count the ways of His faithfulness until we lose track of numbering His gifts. Joy rains down from my eyes, watering the dusty ground. There are no words.

My mind flashes back to another aside of my early teen years. "Papa, one day I want to see a nation be born. I want to be there to be a part of its birth."

Who asks such a thing? Did He, knowing I would be here tonight for the birth of the Republic of South Sudan, put this most unlikely of requests in my heart almost twenty years earlier when I scarcely knew what I asked? All I can think is that truly He does give us the desires of our hearts, puts

His desires in us so that we can ask Him for ther
in turn can delight us with His answers.

I am sitting in Hai Sopiri, Yei, *South* Sudan, tonight in tnꞓ
middle of history being written. I am sitting with a miracle
nation being birthed into being all around me. I am sitting
in the middle of answered prayer humbled by the honor of
receiving His faithful kindness.

When I sat down in my simple bush bungalow to have
my cup of tea and pour out some prose to share with you, I
didn't expect such a divine interruption.

Living in the supernatural reality you were created for is
not just about visits to another realm. It is about the reality
of His realm shifting ours, making history happen all around
us. I could not be more aware of heaven's nearness than I am
in this moment called now in this place called here.

Memories of Forever

Every encounter has a context. A before, a during and an
after. Stories do not exist outside of context. Neither do
encounters. Encounters, those God-meetings, God-moments
breathing life into us all happen in the middle of our daily
story with Him.

Dawn had not yet come on the day this part of my story
began. I was seven.

For me, life came early. So did growing up.

We gathered our things to leave the house; sleep still clung
to my eyes. Another surgery today. There would be 23 al-
together in my first thirteen years.

Mom backed our newly purchased 1983 Park Avenue out of
the garage into the humid Florida darkness—the air replete

with night. I still remember. Plush burgundy swallowed me whole, streetlights blurred as the *thump-thump-thump* of rotating wheels wooed me back into a hesitant sleep.

I woke. Standing before two overgrown glass doors, a white-clad carnival prepared to wrap me in its rush. I teetered at the precipice of adulthood. Innocence peered over the edge with child-eyes.

Polished linoleum, flat fluorescent lights, gleaming chromium bars reflected back this sterile world and pierced me through again. With trepidation I inhaled the familiar sting of ammonia, having returned for more cutting, more mending, more making whole that which was born broken.

My parents should both be nominated for sainthood. Mom never left my side. Fighting with nurses, stalwartly, she refused them tearing her screaming child (me) out of her arms until her little girl was steeled and ready. Waiting long hours in windowless rooms with hushed voices. Sleeping, or not sleeping, in upright chairs for days, weeks on end. Meantime, Dad held the fort, working late hours and creatively figuring out how to remove obstacles that might disable me when I returned home.

The ritual of my growing years: stuffed animals sent in to surgery, company for the places where saint-like parents were rarely allowed, teddy bears robed in green scrubs and masks waited for my waking again.

I slept. I woke. Pain, its four letters seared through my skin and sinew where confused organs were set right. But then, all I knew was pain. How could something so good be so hard?

Death, defeat stared me down and I stared back. I won, but not without leaving part of my innocence behind in the fight.

Just before those hospital doors closed on another chapter of my growing up too soon, heaven's doors opened, and God's love crashed into my seven-year-old world in an encounter I would never recover from.

I had no theology. I had only a heart cry.

I tossed. I turned. The sheets lay like lead on my skin, a Dumbo-sized elephant of dread sat squarely on my chest.

I overheard. I did not mean to listen. But the words found my ears.

They played over and over and over again.

"We have to be prepared for the worst. There's a chance she might die."

Fear found me, blackening the darkness of my bedroom a few nights before I would be admitted to the hospital for this upcoming surgery; breath came long and hard against its weight. I whimpered and wondered.

What would happen if I die? What would happen if I put head to pillow never to wake again? What if? An adult question ripped my child world apart.

Into this context, Jesus, the God-man who defeated death once for all, came.

Nebulous images, faded photos from an old scrapbook of memories you couldn't quite place. They stood just on the edge of my grasp; these stories I had heard about Jesus— healing sick bodies, welcoming children others shooed away.

A cry welled up within, spilled over and split the night.

"Jesus, if You are really real, I want to know You."

The blackness in my room parted. Into this tear in the dark, He came.

He looked nothing like I had seen in storybooks. No paltry, pale-faced Caucasian, He was medium build, with a Middle

Eastern complexion and dark, wavy hair pierced through with gold. Fear vanished before Him. Jesus. He is Love.

His eyes captured me, bottomless blue-green wells of eternity, perfectly placed mosaic irises, colors all dancing together in His light. Fire-love pierced my night and laid me bare, peeling layers of dread away. Truth burgeoned within:

You. Are. Real.

His gaze peered deep, washed deep, wrapping around my heart and calling me into the forever in His gaze.

Then the impossible happened: I was pulled though His gaze right into heaven.

For years it seemed too wildly surreal, but I knew it to be true. For years I had no words, but in recent days these words have found me. So I continue.

Will you come explore with me? This may be my story, but it is your invitation.

Where Are You Sitting?

But before I continue with my experience of heaven, I sense some questions may be stirring within you. Your questions are important to me. And to Him. Questions are wonderful, as long as we hang them on Jesus. Let's pause from this story and then talk about a few things.

I hear accounts of God radically breaking into people's worlds, meeting them where they least expect. Often I hear about the encounter but not the story it is woven into. I hear and I wonder. On what canvas of circumstance is its substance painted? What did it cost to live out the promise it contains? What did it feel like? What did it smell like? How has the sight of heaven changed the person's lens of earth? How did this Word encountered become a Word enfleshed?

Perhaps, my friend, you are wondering what I mean when I say I was pulled into heaven. How is this even biblical?

Let's take a look at Ephesians 2:4–6:

> But God, being rich in mercy, because of His great love with which He loved us, even when we were dead in our transgressions, made us alive together with Christ (by grace you have been saved), and raised us up with Him, and seated us with Him in the heavenly places in Christ Jesus.
>
> NASB

Okay, that is nice for Paul, but what does it really mean for us two millennia later?

That is such a good question. I can only offer my understanding of it all. Each year I spend with my children in Sudan, the more simplified my journey with Jesus becomes. The children teach me to take God's promises as true and real and, by faith, to experience them for myself. Maybe that is why Jesus said that unless we become like little children, we cannot enter the kingdom and experience it for ourselves (see Matthew 18:3).

I did a little word study that taught me some amazing things about that promise in Ephesians 2. It was written all in the past tense. *Made* alive, *raised* up, *seated* with. That means it has already been done in Him. It is finished. It is not only for some future time afar off; it is a reality now.

So tell me. If you were to stop reading this sentence for just a moment and look around the place you are seated in, what do you see? Can you see the color of the walls, the knickknacks on the shelves? Can you touch the chair you are seated in and feel its texture? Can you get up, walk across the room and turn the lights on and off?

Why, dear reader, can you interact so fully with the room you are seated in? Because you are seated *in* the room, right?

I have found many people waiting for heaven to arrest them and yank them into an encounter. I have been one of those. And that can and does happen. But, beloved, you are *already* seated in heavenly places. I am *already* seated there. Do you believe that? Does it make you excited? It does me!

Sometimes we are waiting for Jesus to come down here, when He has invited us to come up there and then bring heaven back down with us. "Come up here," Jesus told John (Revelation 4:1). What an invitation!

I believe this means I don't have to wait. If I am with Jesus, seated with Him in the heavenly places, then I have full and legal access through Him to encounter everything that belongs to Him.

So how does that work? Well, how does anything operate in God's kingdom? By faith.

"Now faith," said Paul, "is the assurance of things hoped for, the conviction of things not seen" (Hebrews 11:1, NASB).

You gave your life to Jesus by faith. You received His gifts of life and freedom by faith. Stepping into this reality of grace is again by faith. Faith is the currency of God's kingdom.

We'll talk more about the *how* in a few pages. For now, I simply want you to know that whether you have experienced any of this for yourself yet or not, in Jesus, you, too, are seated in the heavenly places. Why? Because God says you are. And that is enough. It is true.

Shall I continue and tell you a bit more of the story?

Snapshots of Eternity

As this fearful seven-year-old looked long into Jesus' eyes, my bedroom faded away. I was sitting with Him in a daisy field, legs crossed. Legs. Two legs. There are no crutches in heaven. All that is broken here is whole there.

As I thought about running, I found myself running. There is no lag between thought and execution. "As he thinks in his heart, so is he" (Proverbs 23:7). Jesus watched me, a sparkle in His eyes, as I tried out two legs for the first time.

Many have asked me, "If you really met Jesus, why didn't He give you two legs right then?" My answer is that He did. All that we see here is not all that is real.

I looked out across these grace fields—colors purer than I had ever seen. Radiant, these flowers swayed, bowed, bent their heads low in response to an unseen wind of worship. Jesus picked me up and we spun and we spun. Petals became butterflies swooping in on us—like the butterflies I would see with Him later, as a teenager.

I was spinning until all became a blur except His smile. Slowing, He set me down on sand.

Dunes of glistening grains, catching light, giving it back again. Sands with weight, with purpose I could actually feel as we walked through them. Each grain held a moment, a story treasured in the heart of God. I wanted to sit with Jesus and listen to each one.

We walked until we met a vast sea where eternity washed these sands of time. Its beach dotted with ivory pyramids, empires eroded away by the waves of forever like sandcastles succumbing to a rising tide. Would that be what would happen to what we build around us? Then what would remain?

The scene faded, ebbed, flowed, melded. I stood with Jesus as we appeared to be watching time's first dawn. He smiled, wordlessly showing me the answer to my question.

He seemed to be hovering, brooding. Light shattered darkness with one "Let there be." Time did not exist. Worlds and seas crashed in symphonic release. Darkness set ablaze with destiny, pregnant with purpose, finally to explode forth in the exact expression of God's heart. One word from the lips of love was enough to ignite time, call forth the eternal now to manifest and send planets swirling into place.

He was before it all, and after all passes, He will remain. Jesus. He took me to many places in this heaven realm.

Dear reader, I wonder how this all sounds to you. Do you think it's strange? Is it a bit out there? Or does it make you hungry to know Him more? Again, I am only offering an invitation. This is simply part of my story. God has a unique way of writing all of our stories before one of them comes to be. And they are all different.

The biggest point for me wasn't the experience itself. Even writing this story decades later, I can still barely comprehend it. What did I see? How can I know? But I turned from the scenes before me to look back into Jesus' eyes.

He looked long, looked deep beyond my skin to where I really lived inside. He showed me His hand, scarred still from His own earth walk two millennia before, scarred by His love for me. This seven-year-old knew He had died on the cross in my place. Now He gently put His hand over my heart. My heart leapt as life flowed from His broken place into mine.

I know my natural eyes will never let me see the fullness of what He had to give. But His "more" became a seed planted in the subterranean reaches of my soul. Tiredness crept over me, a soft blanket wrapped around all my questions. I had so many. I still do. Eyelids sagged.

I opened my eyes to find myself back in my room, sitting on my bed. His gaze still focused in eye-to-eye encounter.

He whispered life promises into the nucleus of my tomorrow—embryonic dreams that started forming the very moment He breathed the words into my being.

"What dreams?" you ask. The dreams of seeing people in faraway places come to know who He is. The dreams I am continuing to live out right now.

Heaven Is a Real Place

Even with this incredible experience as my starting place with Jesus, I *still* had to go on a journey of learning how to know His voice every day. A journey filled with questions and cow fields. It is a journey I am still traveling. This adventure of knowing more of Him never ends!

It is one thing when Jesus, in His mercy, crashes into our realm to encounter us in the place of our need. It is quite another to learn how to walk with Him in His realm each and every day.

It is my prayer that as we walk together through these pages, you and I, you will find tools to do just that . . . and that your world will never be the same.

Heaven is a very real place. It is not a theological construct or religious metaphor; it is not simply nice pictures or imaginary figments. It is a place more real than the dusty earth beneath my chair in Yei, South Sudan, tonight. And it is closer to me than the air I breathe.

My experience with heaven when I was seven was profound. But fully understanding the deep reality of what I experienced has taken decades. There was a gap of several years before I even knew I could talk with Jesus every day. Spending time with Him, I slowly began to realize this supernatural life was not going to just "happen." I was called to persist and persevere, to press into His promise until it began to be unleashed around me.

In 1999, I had just finished university. Plans I made, labored long for, fell in one large unceremonious heap in front of me. Shards of my heart were still somewhere in the mix yet to be found from where it had shattered from the fall.

In the middle of all of this, I was preparing to leave my little cupcake-yellow house with white-icing trim and drive seven hours west into flat-landed tornado alley to speak at a small country church. I was going to drive all those hours to share at one service, only to turn around and come straight back the next day.

A whisper came just before my leaving: *Clear your schedule. You will be there for one week.*

"God? Is this You?"

Silence. I knew it was. He need not reply. So I did. And, schedule cleared, I drove. Green hills of east Texas morphed into the open windswept plains of the Panhandle. Seesawing oil drills and skyscraper silos peppered the distant horizon.

Seven hours flew by under the tread of my tires. The late afternoon sun blazed bright, casting long shadows that welcomed me in. I had arrived. Even I could not get lost in this town. It only had one main road and two stoplights. The petite woman pastor stepped out from her storefront church and motioned me to follow.

I stayed the night with this pastor-mom and her family in their turn-of-the-century Victorian-style farmhouse without a farm.

Morning dawned early. One meeting was all that was planned. We turned up to an empty room. Maybe seven people, four under the age of twelve, trickled in.

"Michele, you lead worship, right?"

My eyes wide, I just looked at her. She wasn't asking me; she was telling me. My stomach dropped to my knees. My world began to spin.

What? I did not come for this. I don't lead worship. I know three chords and have no rhythm. Jesus, what have You gotten me into? Help! I will do this only if You come. If You don't come, I am running home.

Reluctantly, I sat down behind six octaves of black and white keys daring me to touch them, desperate prayers careening through my mind. Voices from my past screamed, "You're off-key! Off beat! That note is flat." One man tried to play drums. Three bars in, he gave up. That did not bode well.

Refusing the compulsion to escape out the back door, I squeezed my eyelids tight, put fingers to one ivory chord and sustained. New chord, this one with an ebony note and sustained. Back to the ivories, again sustained.

All at once He came. Three chords in, He came. I could feel water rising up to my knee. A flood in the Texas Panhandle. How? But I was sure my leg was very wet. I felt the water physically rising. I opened my eyes. Nothing visible, but everything invisible.

The rising stopped, beckoned me in. It took me a little while to understand what was happening. I remembered Ezekiel 47 and the river from God's throne. Revelation slammed into my spirit. *Could it be? If this river only rises knee-deep, then I will lie on my face in it. I will dive lower than my knees.*

I abandoned ebony and ivory for carpet and tears. As I lay there, a rain of my own making was soaking the floor. Then He came. Glory fell thick. Two hours later we looked as if we had been subjected to a glitter spill of pandemic proportions. One meeting became seven.

It was good I cleared my schedule for the week. We never topped twelve in number, but Jesus still comes for the twelve.

One day, in between meetings, we piled into the car, the pastor, her daughter and her red-haired son, who I will call Adam—every inch of him a prophet in the making. I had heard that he had seen heaven six years before, when he was three. I wondered what he had seen since then.

I turned in my seat, looked straight into his blue-green eyes and said, "Adam, tell me about when you saw heaven."

He met my gaze head-on, weighing his words. I was not looking into the eyes of a nine-year-old, but someone much older.

"Well," he said slowly, "there's this field. Jesus took me there for my birthday one year. It's one of my favorite places. The colors are different than any here. It is filled with flowers. . . ."

My spirit jumped up inside of me. Suddenly I was seven again.

I interrupted, blurted out, "And they turn into butterflies, right?"

"Yeah." He looked a little surprised. "And there's this beach. . . ."

"The sand has weight, like time, right?"

"Yes." He paused, looking even more surprised. "And Jesus rides a white horse. . . ."

"Lightning?" I interjected. "Sometimes Thunder, the darker one, comes too."

And so for fifteen minutes, we swapped stories, finishing each other's sentences like two people who just discovered they shared a favorite vacation destination. Then realization dawned. His freckled cheeks smiled. His deep, blue-green eyes flashed brightly. He replied with a revelation that pierced me through.

"Hey, you've been there, too!"

I was stunned. Pastor-Mom pulled over. God filled the car with liquid glory. We could not speak or drive. So we sat, all speech yanked right out of us. Pastor-Mom wept.

My mind flashed back to years before when I was still in high school.

I did not even realize it was a prayer. It was a sigh, an aside. I am so grateful that God notes our asides, the sighed prayers of life.

I pulled my new-to-me mauve Pontiac into my family's garage one afternoon after school. As that familiar "I'm home" feeling settled in around me, I let out breath pent up from the day in a barely spoken cry: *God, I want heaven to feel like my garage. I want it to be familiar like my home. I want memories there before I ever arrive permanently.*

I remembered the experience when I was seven, but its images were more like faded snapshots. I grew up. I had grown very logical. Soon after I prayed that prayer in my garage, I began to revisit some of those images again as I spent my daily time with Jesus.

I reasoned perhaps they were nice pictures, maybe metaphors or allegories. I had no idea I was seeing literal places in the Spirit, in the heavenly realms.

Adam was still looking at me, making well sure I got what he said.

Smiling, again he repeated even more slowly, pointedly, his gaze never wavering. "You have *been there, too.*"

The second time he was making a deliberate declaration that still echoes in my spirit.

In the middle of the land of tumbleweed and tornadoes, a nine-year-old freckled prophet taught me that heaven is indeed a very real place, and I had been there more often than I knew.

The Doorway of Testimony

When I share with you, my new friend (at least I hope you will be that), the ways Jesus and I walk together on these unpaved roads of life, the only reason I share them is because the testimony of Jesus *is* the spirit of prophecy (see Revelation 19:10).

Whenever you hear or read of someone else's experience of Jesus, it can become a doorway into one of your own. Why do we give testimony of healings in healing meetings? It is not just because they build people's faith. That is part of it, but it runs far deeper than this alone.

In the supernatural realm, when someone shares a testimony of what Jesus has done or is doing for them, that testimony opens a doorway for everyone who hears to step into an experience with Jesus in a similar way. As Bill Johnson said on Twitter the other day, "A testimony is a legal precedent."

So when I share my experiences with Jesus with you, friend, everything you read is an open door into your own experience with Him.

When you read of angelic encounters and prophetic experiences of the Word in Scripture, these, too, can be gateways of experiencing more of Him and His supernatural world.

Practical Keys: Understanding Access

After these things I looked, and behold, a door standing open in heaven, and the first voice which I had heard, like the sound of a trumpet speaking with me, said, "Come up here, and I will show you what must take place after these things." Immediately I was in the Spirit; and behold, a throne was standing in heaven, and One sitting on the throne.

Revelation 4:1–2, NASB

As I mentioned above, one of the first things we must understand about access is that we have it! Once we realize that we have an open invitation, there are a few practical insights that have really helped me in my journey that I would love to offer to you as nuggets for your own adventure in Him.

We Are Adopted

For you did not receive the spirit of bondage again to fear, but you received the Spirit of adoption by whom we cry out, "Abba, Father."

Romans 8:15

I learn every day from my children the power of this truth. There is a literal Spirit of adoption. I watch it transform little broken lives from the inside out. Adoption opens up for us the assurance of belonging. We belong in Father's house. We have access as His children to explore the heavenly places where we are seated in Christ. We are not trespassing.

Our journey here in Sudan has many bumps and twists. Each one is a lesson in its own way. All reminding me love costs something. His love cost Him everything to bring me home.

Not too long ago, one of my adopted daughters ran away. I breathed silent prayers and prepared to ride into the sunset in search of her. Just as I was about to set out on the back of a motorbike into the night, a call came from one of the members of our team.

"We have her. We prayed. God led us right to her." Tears ran hot as gratitude splashed from my eyes. His love is *so* supernatural.

I waited for their return. Not in my house. At the gate. I would run to meet this one to wrap up her pain, her anger, her fear in my arms. Redemption, our aptly named small, silver four-by-four, bounced in our entrance.

A wilted little girl shuffled out the rear door into my embrace. I spoke truth soft and straight. Slowly, over cups of tea punctuated by sobs, the story spilled, the pain with it. There is no fear in love, for fear has torment. This is the beauty of adoption, of belonging.

She reminded me of the price of Love. What it costs me is a pittance compared to what it cost my Papa in heaven to bring me home when I was running into the night. The love of Jesus was so big He laid down His life so I could come home.

And if He paid such a high price to bring me home, do I not have full access to all He is and has? If He paid such a price for you, beloved reader, how is it that He would withhold the very reality He died to bring you into? Not someday in the sweet by-and-by, but right here in the dusty, messy here and now.

> He who did not spare his own Son, but gave him up for us all—how will he not also, along with him, graciously give us all things?
>
> Romans 8:32, NIV

You have *full* access to all Jesus is and has, and, dear one, it is His good pleasure to give you the kingdom. All of it.

Embrace Hunger As a Gift

> "Blessed are those who hunger and thirst for righteousness, for they shall be filled."
>
> Matthew 5:6

I am convinced. Hunger is a gift. And it is a gift to be guarded. Hunger draws us heavenward. One thing I notice on my travels out of Africa is how much everything in our fast-paced Western world fights against this reality.

I am encouraged to numb it, tame it, ignore it, run from it, deny it, rebuke it . . . do everything but embrace it and cherish it for the incredible gift that it is. Hunger is the one thing I have to fight the hardest to keep alive and growing inside of me when I am back in the West. And make no mistake: spiritual hunger is a love gift, a pure grace from Jesus.

Please, allow me to clarify. I am not talking about striving, make-it-happen works masquerading as hunger. That is spiritual performance, not hunger. I am talking about the lovesick longing for more of the One who is infinite and eternal yet manifest and present in my now. This is the true

59

spiritual hunger that opens our hearts to receive what Jesus wants to give us.

Hunger is not necessarily evidence of a diminished reality of God's presence in my life. It is rather evidence of an increased capacity where Papa has reached down and enlarged my heart to contain more of His. The differential between what I have and what I now have room for is experienced as hunger for Him.

Hunger is what propels us onward in God. Each day I want my capacity for Him to be enlarged, so I pray to be hungrier today than I was yesterday. It is THIS being in constant touch with my need of Him that keeps me pressing in for more understanding and experience of the heavenly places I am seated in. Hungering after His righteousness allows His kingdom to move powerfully wherever I am. Heaven comes to those who know their need, and not just in Africa.

Step In by Faith

Now faith is the substance of things hoped for, the evidence of things not seen.

Hebrews 11:1

When we don't have hope, it is impossible to have faith. We must first have an expectation to hang our faith on. Faith is the currency of God's kingdom.

But practically, what does this mean for us as we seek to encounter the reality of where we are seated in heaven?

When I was a little girl, there was a Bible cartoon series called *Superbook*. These children would get sucked into a Bible story and have incredible exploits in its pages. I loved *Superbook* growing up. It taught me far more than just the major stories of the Bible. It taught me how to engage more actively with Scripture.

One of my favorite questions to ask the Holy Spirit has been, "What do You want to teach me today?" One day He asked if I remembered *Superbook*. He explained that each story, each word of Scripture, is itself an invitation to enter into and explore its reality.

So I decided to give it a try.

I turned over to John's account of the feeding of the five thousand and read the description. Suddenly instead of being black and white letters on a page, the letters became paintbrushes on the canvas of my imagination, my mind's eye.

I could hear the low rumble of the crowd and feel the sun hot on my head. I saw the chagrin on the disciples' faces when Jesus motioned for them to serve up dinner for the masses. Then this little boy with a little lunch was all but overlooked. I saw the twinkle in Jesus' eyes as He bowed low and whispered something that made this little guy burst into a very satisfied grin.

What started as a picture in my imagination became a doorway into an encounter I could step into and walk around in. The same verses we so often quote without a second thought can become our greatest doorways into encountering Him. All it takes is a step of faith.

May I pray for you?

Father, I ask right now You would envelop the one reading these words with Your presence. You would show him or her about the realities of the heavenly realms where we are seated in Christ Jesus. Show him, show her where they are seated in the heavenly places. Come in like a flood

*and begin to open their understanding even more to these
things. Pour out Your Spirit of adoption by which we call
You Abba, Papa, Daddy God. In Your great love, erase any
doubt that full and total access belongs to them, right now
in Christ Jesus, Amen.*

Discussion Questions and Activation Exercise

- Where are you sitting right now? Can you describe your
  surroundings? And where are you also sitting right now
  according to Ephesians 2? Ask Jesus to show you your
  surroundings there, too.
- Remember one time God encountered you. What kind
  of context surrounded that encounter? Did it bring a
  change in your life? What was that change?
- What does Ephesians 2:4–6 mean to you? Ask the Holy
  Spirit to teach you about it.
- What does it mean when Jesus says it is the Father's
  pleasure to give us His kingdom?
- How can you cultivate the gift of hunger in your own
  life?
- What are some things in the supernatural life you are
  hoping for? Verbalizing your hope allows you to have
  something to invest your faith into.
- Ask Jesus to show you something in heaven. Write down
  what you see. If you are having a problem seeing anything, don't worry because we will talk more about
  that in the next chapter. But for now take a peek at
  Revelation 4 and let the account of the throne room be
  painted on the screen of your mind. Don't be surprised

if it becomes an experience you can step into. This is, after all, where you are already seated.

Activation: Practice experiencing your favorite Bible passages. Invite the Holy Spirit to take you into them. Let the words become paintbrushes that fill the canvas of your imagination with pictures. Embrace them and explore a bit with Him. It may initially feel like a daydream, but it really is so much more. Write down what you learn.

3

Gateways to Encounter

I am nine years old, and all I want to be able to do is sing like Julie Andrews. Nine years of a steady diet of show tunes and musicals feed my desire.

But I have one little problem. I am deaf in my left ear and cannot hear well enough to even properly pronounce some of my words, let alone carry a tune.

One morning I sit in our sweet little Anglican church in northeast Florida. Baby doll clutched in my arms, I perch on the hard wooden pew. Hot salty liquid leaks from my eyes. My focus is singular. I want to sing in the choir. It does not bother me that they do not have a children's program. I want to sit in the big people's choir with the robes and the folders all standing at attention. I know I, too, have a song.

My mother, ever my champion, agrees to join the choir just for me. And thus begins our weekly ritual of choir practice and Sunday morning service. For the next eight years I will grow up in the choir loft.

It is not an easy eight years. I am out of tune for probably six of them. Everyone is incredibly gracious to a tenacious little girl who knows she has a song buried deep inside.

The patience of our choir leader, a retired musician, helps me find my key. In a stroke of genius, she sits me right next to the back of the piano. I eventually learn to feel the note more than hear it. There is a resonance when the note you sing matches the notes of the song. When the notes match, you can literally feel it.

I don't realize until much later that my short-lived and sporadic musical career is not about music at all. It is about learning how to hear, how to connect. It's about learning how to allow a sensory area that is weak to be honed and trained by use of practice. Learning how to listen and receive not with my ears alone, but with my whole being.

And just as in the natural, our spiritual senses come alive when we invest time and effort into allowing the Holy Spirit to train and tune them to His sound, to His song, to His way of seeing.

Our Spiritual Senses

As I mentioned earlier, I am privileged to care for well over one hundred beautiful sons and daughters of all ages. One of my favorite age groups to be with (if I am allowed to have favorites) are my two- to three-year-olds.

They are brimming with their own little personalities and are just beginning to discover the world around them on their own. How I want to be like them when I grow up: all wonder-washed and amazed by the simplest things. And while they are discovering this world, they have not yet forgotten the eternity from which they came.

I watch sheer amazement cross their little faces as they chase butterflies and watch seeds emerge as small green leaves from the hidden depths of the earth; when they have their first-ever marshmallow cooked over a roaring fire and warm, sweet gooeyness squishes in their mouths as delight brightens their eyes. I watch them enjoy every inch of their world, each of their senses fully engaged, completely alive both in this realm and the unseen realm of God's kingdom.

We learn early on we have five senses: touch, taste, sight, smell and hearing. That seems simple enough. These are the gateways by which we experience the natural world all around us. But what someone usually forgets to tell us is that we have spiritual senses God created to be just as active and alive as our natural ones.

How do we interact with His supernatural realm? Through our spiritual senses!

The Scriptures themselves testify to the importance of these in our life with God:

> Oh, taste and see that the LORD is good; blessed is the man who trusts in Him!
>
> Psalm 34:8

> I was in the Spirit on the Lord's Day, and I heard behind me a loud voice, as of a trumpet. . . . Then I turned to see the voice that spoke with me.
>
> Revelation 1:10, 12

> Now thanks be to God who always leads us in triumph in Christ, and through us diffuses the fragrance of His knowledge in every place.
>
> 2 Corinthians 2:14

> Then one of the seraphim flew to me, having in his hand a live coal which he had taken with the tongs from the altar. And he touched my mouth with it, and said: "Behold, this has touched your lips; your iniquity is taken away, and your sin purged."
>
> Isaiah 6:6–7

And these senses can be trained by practice.

> But solid food belongs to those who are of full age, that is, those who by reason of use have their senses exercised to discern both good and evil.
>
> Hebrews 5:14

I don't know about you, but to me this is amazing news. It means I am not stuck in the level of revelation and understanding I currently walk in. Just as when I was nine behind the piano in the choir loft, even one of my weakest senses could be trained with the right instruction and practice.

The more I practice what God has given me, the more my senses, both natural and spiritual, are exercised by reason of use and can be honed and refined by Him.

Unless, that is, I am experiencing some kind of hindrance.

Dealing with Blocked Senses

Do you ever have a nagging sense that receiving from God is just plain difficult for you?

Sometimes, just as a physical doorway might be blocked from being opened, the gateways of our spiritual senses might be blocked, too. Before we go any further, I want to share with you what some of those blockages are and how we can deal with them.

Let's talk specifically about the eye "gate," the place of vision. Why is it called a gate? A gate is an entrance point, in this case, information in the form of visual images. It is also a point of decision. You can open the gate to receive the images or shut the gate to reject them. Sometimes there are things that stand in the way of our being able to receive what God wants to show us. This hindrance is what I mean by a blocked eye gate.

Of all the five spiritual senses, the place of vision is the one area I have the most experience in. It is not only how I most often connect and receive from God, it is also one of the places the enemy has tried his hardest to shut down in my life. But the same principles we are about to discuss for the eye gate can be applied to any of the sensory gateways that God reveals Himself through.

"Blessed are the pure in heart, for they shall see God."

Matthew 5:8

The eyes we are speaking of primarily are not our physical eyes but our spiritual ones, the eyes of our heart. Blessed are the ones whose hearts are pure, innocent, clean and undefiled. Anything that causes impurity or mixture in our hearts can cloud and confuse our vision. As you can imagine, the list here could be very long!

But for the sake of our conversation, let's just touch on four main areas that can cause problems in our ability to see accurately.

1. Lacking a Mental "Grid"

One of the biggest hindrances to actively engaging the supernatural realm is either not knowing we can or not knowing that it is even there. Much of this comes from what we haven't been taught as much or more than what we have been taught. Some have called this our paradigm. I like to call it our *grid*.

We all have one. The only way we form new memories is by associating them with old ones. If I have no point of reference of something as real or important, if I have no place to put it within my grid, my brain literally filters it as nonessential information, hits delete and sends it to the trash bin of its computer filing system.

In other words, if I don't have a grid for something, my brain will not retain it even if my eyes "see" it. How sobering is that?

That is one of the reasons we have to be "transformed by the renewing of [our] mind" (Romans 12:2). Literally, that phrase means that our minds are changed into another form, as our comprehension and our ability to perceive, understand and remember are made completely new.

How do we create a new mental grid? One way is through the Scriptures. The Bible is filled with encounters and stories that give us pictures of what God's supernatural kingdom is like. We need to spend time there, just lingering and letting God use the images He has already given us to inform and transform our mental grids, so that our minds are better able to contain the revelation He wants to show us.

A few other ways we can create a new mental grid are by activity associations (we will talk about those in a few pages), proactively spending time each day with Jesus listening to Him and keeping a record of the promises He gives us. You can also create a new mental grid by asking God questions as He shows you things. It is all about relationship, and He delights to give you the kingdom. The more we actively engage what He gives us, the more our mental grid stretches and transforms.

2. Destructive Visual Images

We live in a media image-driven world. Even if you don't want to see less than wholesome images, they are sometimes really hard to avoid.

I remember being ten or eleven and spending the night at a neighborhood sleepover. Innocent enough, right? What could eight little girls possibly get into?

Sleepovers included movies. Visual imagery and stories are powerful things. And since I am a visual, kinesthetic learner, their impact for me personally is greatly intensified. You can tell me one hundred times, and I might *possibly* remember. But if you show me a picture, it is embedded so deeply in my file system that it takes Jesus to delete it. I am convinced that is why He shows me things as much or more than He tells me them. He is intimately "acquainted with all my ways" (Psalm 139:3), and that includes my natural learning styles.

The movie on schedule that night was a real scare fest. *Poltergeist.* Do you remember that horror film from 1982? It is the stuff night terrors are made of. I think I was scared of my closet for years. Those images haunted me.

We have to be so, so careful if we want to see accurately, in order that the eyes of our hearts are not clouded over with other images. We may think images do not affect us: the sex, the violence, the supernatural dark side invading our media world today. Movies are not bad in themselves; they are mar-velous tools of communication and can even be prophetic. But the demonically inspired subject matter of some of their content can be troublesome.

71

May I encourage you to consider taking a visual fast of sorts? Think about a break from bombardment by television, movies and media imagery just for 21 days. Spend that time asking Jesus to sort out the images in your mental filing cabinet. He is not shocked, upset or disappointed in any inappropriate ones that got stuck there. He was watching it all with you the first time it got filed.

> There is therefore now no condemnation to those who are in Christ Jesus, who do not walk according to the flesh, but according to the Spirit.
>
> Romans 8:1

I have found with images I need to get rid of that they will never go when I just ignore them. That pushes them away from the light and farther back into the darkness, where they continue to lurk—only to reemerge later. The only way they will truly be erased from the eyes of my heart is for me to embrace them and bring them to Jesus, who is the light. When they are released to Him, He removes them as far as east is from west.

Truth be told, I cannot remember a single image from that movie that was so terrifying at the time. His blood has literally deleted that file. Forever.

3. Inner Vows

I was twelve or thirteen. I was in one of the stalls in the church bathroom during a youth retreat. I heard two girls come in and start talking about how they could invoke a demonic being in the mirror by turning the lights off, twirling so many times and chanting its name. When it appeared, they said, it would try to harm the one who had invoked it.

I had heard other girls in school talking about this "game" as well. I could feel my heart begin thumping inside my chest. Because of my own journey, I took the unseen realm very seriously.

Then the girls in the restroom began to imagine how "fun" it would be to lock someone in after this creature had been summoned, just to see what would happen.

Until that point the girls had been unaware of my presence. I stood frozen behind the stall door, terrified at the thought that they might realize I was there and subject me to their experiment.

Well, they must have turned and noticed my foot cemented in place. Suddenly, I heard them giggle and whisper something. And the next thing I knew, the light switched off, and I was left alone in pitch-dark nothingness.

I had no idea at that time that in Jesus the demonic has no power. The icy fingers of fear slithered up my back. My mouth tasted like cotton mixed with bile, and I squeezed my eyes shut hard. "I don't want to see it. I never want to see. Please let there be nothing there."

I fumbled desperately with the bolt on the stall door, jerked open the door and scooted through the blackness into the cool night air and bright moonlight beyond.

But the damage had been done. Fear had caused me to make an inner vow not to see. I had given my gift from Jesus over to fear. Period. While what I didn't want to see was the demonic, my vow not to see had the immediate effect of blocking my spiritual sight across the board, of things both good and bad.

God honors our choices. It was not until a few years later, after learning to hear His voice, that I realized I needed to break that vow because it had put a padlock on my ability to see clearly with my spiritual eyes.

It was simple to do. *"Jesus, I am sorry for agreeing with fear and choosing not to see. I am sorry for giving fear my ability to see. I break agreement with my vow and ask Your forgiveness. Please restore my ability to see into Your realm."*

Amen. Done. From that moment on, I began to see again.

4. Occult Practices

Another hindrance to seeing accurately is any experience of the occult that has not been repented of. Often that history comes with images that need to be plunged into the sea of forgetfulness. And almost always there are spiritual ties that need to be broken. For many it is as simple as bringing it all to Jesus and letting Him wash it away, setting them free.

Our media world is so riddled with occult practices that it makes them seem normal, even trendy. Some people who truly love Jesus even get pulled into thinking there is no harm in dabbling in these areas. But any practice that draws its power from darkness is no game.

Occult practice goes far beyond Wicca, Satanism and knowingly engaging in witchcraft. Ouija boards and "spell-casting guides" are marketed now as innocuous children's games. Many people consider séances, tarot cards and horoscopes as entertainment. Vampirism has been made fashionable again by love stories in current young adult literature. Reiki healing and shamanistic ceremonies are often available at upscale trendy health spas and resorts. There is a growing fascination with the very real spiritual world around us.

Even if the occult world is engaged innocently out of ignorance, it can have profound effects on our ability to see clearly in the supernatural. All occult practice, no matter how beautifully packaged, obtains its power from the demonic. Participating with it, even as a form of entertainment, is trading into a demonic agenda and opening up doors for the enemy to cause major havoc in our lives. Satan's ultimate goal is always "to steal, kill and destroy" (John 10:10).

We, as the Body of Christ, need to walk in such love, authority and power that the supernatural demonstration of God's kingdom in our lives draws the hungry and the hurting to Him. Why should living supernaturally be possible only in the bush of Africa? If we are to bring the Good News to a world hungry for spiritual reality, God's supernatural kingdom needs to be flowing through our lives every day, no matter where we live.

I know my deepest journeys of freedom have always been walked out in a safe, loving community.

I encourage you that if there is anything in this area of occult practice that you are still battling, find those who will love you, pray and stand with you for total freedom.

Engaging the Realm of the Kingdom

I have shared many stories in this book so far, and even a few in this chapter, which come from the storehouse of my own journey. All these God meetings and grace pictures are intensely personal treasures. I lay them up like Mary, pondering them in my heart, plucking them from deep within, bringing them carefully into the light.

I am honored to share them with you. But I am writing this book so you, my friend, will not just read about my encounters, but experience your own. So right now let's move in that direction.

Jesus tells us, "The kingdom of God is within you" (Luke 17:21). He also tells us, "The kingdom of heaven is at hand" (Matthew 4:17). His kingdom within and His kingdom without are both closer to us than the air we breathe.

One thing that has helped me greatly in the process of learning how to embrace the kingdom of God within is to create tangible "contact points" for my faith.

Remember how we learn? We need a memory of something already in place on which to hang new information, so we can retain what we experience. Well, sometimes when we don't have a memory in place, God may lead us to create one.

Put your hand up to touch your face. There is a little layer of air between your hand and your face. That is how close the kingdom of heaven is to you right now. If you lean into your hand ever so slightly, that is all the effort it takes to lean into the nearness of God's kingdom.

And then there are the times we just need good old-fashioned reminders to help us stay aware throughout our day of the invitation to walk in God's supernatural kingdom.

> Speak to the children of Israel: Tell them to make tassels on the corners of their garments throughout their generations, and to put a blue thread in the tassels of the corners. And you shall have the tassel, that you may look upon it and remember all the commandments of the LORD and do them.
>
> Numbers 15:38–39

I really appreciate that the ancient Hebrew people were instructed to tie on visible reminders of what God had told them. Why do I appreciate this so much? Because it makes me feel less "other." I, too, need reminding.

Contact Points

One of the ways I have found to encourage and cultivate a continual awareness of God's presence throughout my day is by setting up regular contact points to engage my faith.

Visual, practical reminders are very helpful to me. They are like ongoing object lessons that help keep me aware of Him throughout my day, even when I am easily distracted.

Creative Memory Associations

When I climb into a vehicle and shut the door, for example, it reminds me I am shut into grace and carried by His presence. When I step out, I step out to bring the fullness of His kingdom with me. When I wash my face at night, I am washing off the day and leaving it with Jesus. And so on.

Little activity associations like that help me create places of remembrance and active engagement with His ever-present reality in my daily life. When I remember, I stay aware of how truly close He is.

Communion

One of the greatest contact points I have found in engaging the reality of the supernatural kingdom of God is taking Communion each day. Communion is all about remembering and, in that remembering, becoming.

And He took bread, gave thanks and broke it, and gave it to them, saying, "This is My body which is given for you; do

this in remembrance of Me." Likewise He also took the cup
after supper, saying, "This cup is the new covenant in My
blood, which is shed for you."

Luke 22:19–20

For me Communion extends far deeper than a metaphor
we corporately partake of once a week or once a quarter. It
is more than ceremony and ritual.

"I am the bread of life. Your fathers ate the manna in the
wilderness, and are dead. This is the bread which comes
down from heaven, that one may eat of it and not die. I am
the living bread which came down from heaven. If anyone
eats of this bread, he will live forever."

John 6:48–51

Communion is a living reminder of the body of Jesus broken that my body might be transfigured and made whole. A
reminder of His blood shed that even my DNA, the most
foundational building block of who I am, might be changed
into His likeness. And it is more than a reminder. Communion
is receiving the very life Jesus has inside of Him, so that this
life might become tangibly alive inside of me.

Some Christians believe that we should partake of Communion only in church, only with other believers, rather than
alone; or only as administered by ordained pastors or elders.
I understand these views, but my own journey has led me
personally to different conclusions.

I actively take Communion each day as I sit down to eat
my breakfast, lunch and dinner. These meals in themselves
become Communion to me. Instead of just thanking God
for my food, I take a moment to remember that even that

act of remembering might open a place for me to regularly encounter God throughout my day.

To eat and drink of who Jesus is that I might be changed by His life resonating inside of me changes me from the inside out. It helps me to remember and bring back into focus in the middle of my most natural moments the truth that every day I am called deeper into this supernatural life.

Practical Keys: Setting Your Desire

"If you abide in Me, and My words abide in you, you will ask what you desire, and it shall be done for you."

John 15:7

"Therefore I say to you, whatever things you ask when you pray, believe that you receive them, and you will have them."

Mark 11:24

One of the biggest keys for stepping into the supernatural walk God has for us involves the intentional setting of our desire.

Our desires set up a foundation for the things we desire to manifest. What we desire, we turn in toward. What we turn in toward, we focus on. What we focus on, we empower. What we empower, expands around us. What we behold, we become.

Most of us have probably heard very few if any teachings on how to set our desires. But if we do not actively engage our desires internally, and fix them on things above, there is a good chance our desires will be engaged by the external world around us.

> If then you were raised with Christ, seek those things which are above, where Christ is, sitting at the right hand of God. Set your mind on things above, not on things on the earth.
>
> Colossians 3:1–2

This verse could also be translated, "Set your *desire* on things above." How do we fix our desire above? We set our minds there. The word for *mind* comes from a root word that means the midriff, the seat of feelings and also the understanding. So setting our desire on things above means literally to exercise our minds, to direct our thoughts, to seek after those things that are above.

Thus we exercise our thought lives; we dream about the things we desire to experience with God. And that process of dreaming actually creates a place of expectancy, which can then lead into full-blown faith.

> Hope deferred makes the heart sick, but desire fulfilled is a tree of life.
>
> Proverbs 13:12, NASB

Desire establishes a platform for faith's demonstration. If I don't dream it, I'll never do it. Desire fulfilled is a tree of life. One reason we have so much hope deferred in the Body of Christ is we don't cultivate godly desire. History is birthed in a place of dreaming with God and engaging His desires in the earth.

And when we talk about dreaming and expectancy, I have a confession to make. I am a little bit of an X-Men fan. X-Men is a movie series about a group of superheroes whose genetic DNA code gives them astounding abilities. There is something about all those super-heroic, earth-transforming, villain-nabbing supernatural abilities that calls out to the very DNA of what I am created for. I dream about changing the world.

We read a lot in the Bible about Jesus healing the sick and bringing salvation and deliverance. If we grew up in church, we have heard about those activities most of our lives. We are in some ways just now really getting a grid for that kind of supernatural. But He did so much more.

We casually skip over the parts of Jesus walking through walls (see John 20:19). How else would He get in the room with the door shut? He glowed and turned invisible (see Luke 4:30). Again, how else would He walk right *through* an angry mob bent on killing Him? He heard people's thoughts (see Luke 5:22; 6:8; 11:17), changed weather patterns (see Matthew 8:26; Mark 4:39; Luke 8:24), altered one substance into another (see John 2), walked on water (see John 6:19), trans-relocated (see Luke 24:31; John 6:21) and flew or ascended if you prefer (see Luke 24:51), to name a few!

A list like that makes Him sound like the ultimate X-Man. Evil villains beware. Oh, wait! He already took away your powers on the cross. Be very afraid. I have read the last chapter of the Book. So have you. We win.

This I know, He is the same today as He was yesterday as He will be tomorrow. He has one Body on the earth right now, and we are it. He promised that we would do greater things than these (see John 14:12), but how do we get to "greater" if we aren't even dreaming about walking in these realms as our "normal"?

The lesser-read pages of church history are filled with radical lovers of Jesus walking in similar phenomena as their own "normal." No one batted an eyelash when Saint Francis floated to the tree line in worship, or Saint Joseph of Cupertino flew around the sanctuary.

I really believe Papa wants to pour this level of glory out on the earth—and more. He wants us to walk in the "greater things than these." I know these things are coming, and I want to dive lower and closer to His burning heart to embrace an Enoch walk that spans heaven and earth.

Do you remember Enoch? He is known in the Bible as one who walked so closely with God, that one day he simply "was not." He was translated straight into heaven without dying. But before God took him, Enoch had the testimony of being pleasing to God (see Hebrews 11:5). I want to cultivate the same kind of testimony that comes from supernatural faith developed in the place of deep intimacy with God. We will talk more about Enoch in chapter 7.

Did you ever dream, even when you were little, about having superpowers? Yes, you—reading this with wide eyes and a dirty kitchen floor. Perhaps you have dreamed of them, because in Jesus, it is what you are created for.

May I pray for you?

Papa God, I ask that You would awaken desire in the heart of the one reading right now. Every time this dear heart has been shut down, crushed and disappointed, pour out Your healing, and give him or her courage to dream again with You.

I am asking, Balm of Gilead, that You place eye salve on the eyes of his or her heart and command his or her ears to be open, so that any withered sense of touch would be restored, so that he or she might smell Your fragrance and taste Your goodness. Cause this dear one's senses to be fully alive to You and Your goodness.

I pray just as Paul did for the church in Ephesus that by having "the eyes of your heart flooded with light . . . you can know and understand the hope to which He has called you, and how rich is His glorious inheritance in the saints . . . [so that you can know and understand] what is the immeasurable and unlimited and surpassing greatness of His power in and for us who believe" (Ephesians 1:18–19, AMP).

Remove any blocks or hindrances to perceiving the fullness of what You are showing this dear one reading these words right now. Let those hindrances be removed as far as the east is from the west so that the gateways of his or her spiritual senses would be purified, refined and cleared to receive accurately from You. Amen.

Discussion Questions and Activation Exercise

- Ask the Holy Spirit to bring to mind one specific time you encountered the supernatural realm through your senses. Those little hairs that stand up on the back of your neck when you feel God move in a room, the faintest image fleeting through your mind's eye, the softest whisper of the Holy Spirit's encouragement, one time when those words leapt straight off the page and into your heart . . . or one of a million other ways He comes.

- Spend some time allowing the Holy Spirit to reveal any way your spiritual senses have been shut down or blocked. Talk through these areas with Him; confess agreement with the enemy's lie as what it is—sin; receive forgiveness, and ask Jesus to restore what was stolen.

- What kind of grid do you have for supernatural encounter? Spend some time chewing on the encounters in the Bible and let Jesus redefine or expand your grid.

- How might you actively engage your desire toward this invitation into a supernatural life? What or where do you normally spend your time and energy thinking about most? How might you set your thoughts above?

- If you could have one superpower, what would it be and why?

- Where has your desire been crushed or disappointed? Take those places to Jesus and ask Him to heal them, that your desire might be whole and wholly set on Him.

Activation: You realize that training your senses can take practice, so keep asking, keep knocking and keep seeking. All this belongs to you. It is *your* inheritance in Him. Do you actually believe that?

Pick one normal activity in your day that can serve to remind you about a truth of God's supernatural kingdom. Practice this activity, letting it cultivate your awareness of the Lord's nearness throughout the day. Soon you will find you won't have to "practice" it. You will just be more in touch with Jesus' presence and walking more in the full provision of who He is every day for you.

4

Ten Myths about the Supernatural Life

I am a sophomore in the university. It is my first day of university Bible class, and we are all resolutely encouraged to start our quests to become good Bereans (see Acts 17:10–11). "Be Bereans," we are told by our professor. He continues to give his definition of what he thinks a good Berean is, telling us, "Prove wrong all that is untrue. There is a lot of deception out there. You can't be too careful."

My classes seem intent on disproving the ideas that do not fit in their grid. This, after all, is the scientific method to discerning truth. Form a hypothesis and in a carefully constructed experiment, test it out for all it is worth. If you by chance prove your theory true, it is still in question. Many more in the scientific community must be able to replicate your results, and their sole intent in doing so is to disprove them.

This might be excellent protocol in a lab, but it is absolutely the wrong premise in the kingdom. Unfortunately I am being taught to apply this measure to areas of my faith. In fact, I am told I have swallowed some myths about walking in supernatural reality.

Suddenly my walk with Jesus is being dissected, and the Scriptures I hold on to subjected to scientific scrutiny. I grow confused and am honestly a bit rocked by it all. So I do the one thing I know to do: ask Jesus what He thinks and what He says.

His reply takes me deeper into His heart, even in the middle of an academic environment that seems intent to explain away anything supernatural, anything illogical and anything that requires childlike faith.

"Beloved, be a Berean. But make sure you know what a Berean is and how they studied."

So armed with that instruction, I look into what a Berean was to test out the definition I have been given by my Bible professor.

> Now the Berean Jews were of more noble character than those in Thessalonica, for they received the message with great eagerness and examined the Scriptures every day to see if what Paul said was true.
>
> Acts 17:11, NIV

And thus I learn a very prevalent pitfall: My academic career is teetering on the edge of the danger of a right idea with a wrong premise.

Let me explain a bit more about what I mean by a right idea with the wrong premise before we uncover ten myths about the supernatural life.

Methods of the Kingdom

One of the greatest hindrances to growing in new understandings in our journey can be the way we receive a message contrary to our current understanding. Often we immediately search the Scriptures to find out whether it is false.

That is the scientific method, not the kingdom method.

Jesus tells us to receive the message with great eagerness, like the Bereans, and search the Scriptures to see whether it is true. When we assume falsehood out of a fear of being deceived, we open ourselves inadvertently to interpreting the Scriptures through a spirit of fear and not the leading of the Holy Spirit.

> "However, when He, the Spirit of truth, has come, He will guide you into all truth; for He will not speak on His own authority, but whatever He hears He will speak; and He will tell you things to come."
>
> John 16:13

When we lean into God's Spirit of truth, He will show us if there is something that does not line up with His Word, ways or character. He is more concerned than we are with our getting it right!

A premise based on a spirit of fear is simply a wrong premise in the kingdom.

So please let me encourage you. I am very aware that some of you reading this book might find some of what I am saying a bit out of the box. And that is very okay.

Might I encourage you to be a Berean in all the things that raise questions for you?

I am not asking you to simply accept my perspective—or anyone else's, for that matter. Please go search it out for yourself and let the Holy Spirit instruct you. Receive the message with eagerness and then spend regular time examining the Scriptures with Him to see if what I am saying is true.

Myth Busters

And now we get to those ten myths about the supernatural life. Have you run into some of these myths about walking in the supernatural realities you are created for? They want to steal the invitation of heaven right out of your hands. And that is not okay.

One definition of a myth is *a widely held but false belief or idea*. There are a lot of these floating around about the supernatural life in current-day Christendom. You cannot journey too far without bumping into at least one of them.

When I started out, no one told me there were some potential potholes in the road that would have loved to derail the journey I was on. It might have been enormously helpful to know ahead of time so I would not have to discover so many of them firsthand.

Let's take a look at ten myths about walking in the supernatural. They are in no particular order; and yes, I have at one time or another in my journey fallen into and/or butted against every single one of them.

1. Impressive Gifts Prove Character

I entered the room hesitantly as it filled with people. I was still in university at the time.

There was a visiting speaker who had a reputation for moving with great supernatural power and seeing many people get healed. I was eager to receive all that God had. I even brought friends with me.

As the worship began, I felt an expectation rising in the room. But there was something else I could not put my finger on. Something felt off to me. Still very new to corporate meetings such as this, I checked my reservation and shelved it till later.

The enigmatic speaker I am certain you have likely *never* heard of got up and started a thirty-minute offering preamble. My spirit began to churn. This was not on. It seemed so manipulative. I began to feel sick in the pit of my stomach. But then again . . . I should be giving the benefit of the doubt. Love always hopes. I chided myself for being so judgmental.

The service only went downhill from there. People did get healed in the ministry time, and my friends wanted to go down to the front for prayer from the speaker. But because of some of the things I was sensing, I wanted to go nowhere near whatever was operating. Something felt wrong, but I did not have the understanding to go with what I was picking up.

Long story short, it turned out that even with people getting healed and God honoring people's faith and hunger in these meetings, this speaker had a lot of blatant issues in his life that came out later publicly. My heart felt saddened by it all. Some days you really truly hope you are wrong.

In the first place, spiritual manipulation—which is what I sensed going on in that thirty-minute offering preamble—is basically witchcraft.

And in the second place, as a friend in those days used to say, "Gifts can take you where your character can't keep you." Gifts are given, but character is cultivated. Great gifting is not the measure of someone's closeness to Jesus. Why? Because the gifts and calling of God are irrevocable (see Romans 11:29).

It is easy to be impressed by someone's supernatural gifting. I celebrate the gifts of others, but I refuse to be impressed by anything or anyone but Jesus.

We are known by our fruit, not our gifts. While I eagerly pursue every supernatural gifting God wants me to operate in, my greatest goal is kingdom fruit that remains through an intimate love relationship with Jesus.

2. Don't Judge

"Judge not, that you be not judged" (Matthew 7:1).

How many times have we heard this Scripture phrase quoted? The problem is that it is usually quoted entirely out of context with little to no understanding of what true godly judgment is.

I spent years beating myself up for the things I saw, thinking I was just being judgmental and harsh, trying to shut down the very thing God was trying to grow me in: discernment.

If we are going to walk in the supernatural reality we are created for, we need to understand what God says about discernment and godly judgment.

> "Judge not, that you be not judged. For with what judgment you judge, you will be judged; and with the measure you use, it will be measured back to you. And why do you look at the speck in your brother's eye, but do not consider the plank in your own eye? Or how can you say to your brother, 'Let me remove the speck from your eye'; and look, a plank is in your own eye? Hypocrite! First remove the plank from your own eye, and then you will see clearly to remove the speck from your brother's eye."
>
> Matthew 7:1–5

When we read this passage in context, following verse one with verses two through five, we can see this passage is *not* saying don't judge. It is dealing rather with the context of judgment and the heart attitude behind it.

True judgment for those of us in Christ is about restoration, not destruction. The point is: We have to be willing to judge the plank in our own eye, and let God bring loving restoration to our blighted vision before we can even begin to discern that speck in our brother's eye.

Jesus is warning us that if we do not allow our issues to be judged first inside of Him and allow Him to cleanse us and set us free, then the judgment we issue outside of this reality will come back to bite us.

Why do I include this as a myth about the supernatural life?

An out of context "Don't judge . . ." can put so much fear in us that we shut down the very function of discernment God wants to mature in us and, in effect, shroud our ability to see in the supernatural realm. The pitfall in discernment is not often what we see; usually, it is what we do with what we see.

I will be sharing more on all this in chapter 9 when we speak of kingdom government. It really deserves its own special space.

3. I Could Never Hear God As You Do

Have you noticed how utterly uncreative the enemy of our souls is when it comes to lying to us about our supernatural destinies?

The reason we are taking time in this chapter to debunk his myths, his monsters lurking in the closets of our faith journeys, is that lies have power only when we keep them in the darkness. But when we bring them into the light of God's love, choosing to believe the truth, they rapidly fall apart in front of our eyes.

I am privileged to travel the world roughly one-third of the time to share about my journey. I have had many people come up and tell me that they could never hear God as I do. That makes me sad because it is just not true. What I walk in is available to anyone. How I walk it out and what it looks like might be unique to me, but the realm of revelation and intimacy I walk in is what Jesus died to open for all of us.

When someone comes and says this to me, I often ask them, "Why?" Usually I hear something like:

"I am not special enough."

"I am not anointed enough."

"I don't have a ministry."

Dear reader, have any of these types of thoughts ever tried to lodge in your heart? I have yet to meet anyone who could honestly reply no, myself included. We have all struggled with something in this area at some point in our journey.

Proverbs tells us as a man thinks in his heart, so is he (see Proverbs 23:7) and that death and life are in the power of the tongue (see Proverbs 18:21). We frame our world by the words we speak. We speak out of the overflow of what is in our hearts (see Matthew 12:34). We become what we think in our hearts and then we release it to operate in the world around us by the way we speak.

The Hebrew word for *think* used here literally means "to act as a gatekeeper." That which we allow into our hearts and engage in our thoughts determines what we become.

The deepest battle, therefore, lies in the heart. Even with my history with God, sometimes when I see someone function in an arena I have not engaged in yet, the enemy tries to whisper insecurity to see if he can find a landing pad in my heart.

So I am not immune from his attempts. I just know at times more of what to do with them if they come.

The lies of the enemy are invitations. And not all invitations should be accepted!

When he comes knocking with his lies, I refuse to answer the door or let those lies in. And I let him know in no uncertain terms that it will be on his head if he persists.

4. If I Embrace the Supernatural Side of God's Kingdom, I Might Get a Demon

The demonic world would absolutely love to keep the Body of Christ disconnected from her Head and immobilized by fear about everything in the supernatural world. Again, as I said before, any premise based on a spirit of fear is a wrong premise in the kingdom.

> "If a son asks for bread from any father among you, will he give him a stone? Or if he asks for a fish, will he give him a serpent instead of a fish? Or if he asks for an egg, will he offer him a scorpion? If you then, being evil, know how to give good gifts to your children, how much more will your heavenly Father give the Holy Spirit to those who ask Him!"
>
> Luke 11:11–13

When we are seeking the kingdom of God, and more of the Holy Spirit, out of a place of intimacy and relationship with Jesus, we need not fear we will be sidetracked by the demonic. If you go after supernatural experiences or power outside of relationship with Jesus, on the other hand, you most definitely will engage with the demonic world.

> Jesus said to him, "I am the way, the truth, and the life. No one comes to the Father except through Me."
>
> John 14:6

It is inside of who Jesus is that we find our access to the supernatural destiny for which we were created. It is all about relationship with Him.

When I first started listening to God in my late teens and early twenties, I was really concerned I might follow a wrong voice. I spent hours asking, "Is this me or is this God?" I realized I was rapidly becoming so concerned with engaging a wrong source that I had stopped engaging the right Source.

One day I heard this whisper from Jesus filled with the light of His smile: "Beloved, *stop* trying so hard. Am I big enough to handle your mistakes?"

It really wasn't a question. I then realized Papa God was far more committed to my seeing and hearing accurately than even I was. It wasn't about my always getting it right, but about my growing in relationship with Him.

5. Interaction with the Angelic Is Dangerous

Regular, everyday interaction with the angelic realm is 100 percent absolutely legal and normal in the kingdom of God.

> But to which of the angels has He ever said: "Sit at My right hand, till I make Your enemies Your footstool"? Are they not all ministering spirits sent forth to minister for those who will inherit salvation?
>
> Hebrews 1:13–14

"Those who will inherit salvation" are—if you are in Jesus—us. You and I.

I find it curious why it is so much easier to find books on demons and warfare than it is to find books on angels and how to function with them. There are whole shelves dedicated to demonology and deliverance and how the demonic world operates.

I have yet to find books on the angelic realms of heaven and how they operate in similar detail or abundance. I just find it interesting. I am happy that this trend is beginning to change, though. Recently Judith MacNutt released a whole book called *Angels Are for Real*, dedicated to introducing people to the reality of the angelic in our everyday lives.

What you focus on, you empower. What you lean into, you move toward. What you behold, you become.

I am grateful we have an increased understanding of how the enemy operates, and I definitely do not want to be ignorant of his schemes. My understanding of spiritual warfare, however, is very simple. I show up. God shows off. Darkness moves out, and Jesus wins so I win. Period. It is a done deal.

I do not want to give the devil one second more of my attention than need be. I do not wake up binding every demon I can think of to bind. That would actually be like saying good morning to the demonic world. It would empower it to become the center of my attention. And that is a pleasure I have no intention of giving it!

I wake up in the morning very intentionally saying, "Good morning, Holy Spirit," and greeting, thus acknowledging, the angelic and kingdom realm operating around my life. What you acknowledge, you empower to function around you.

Let no one cheat you of your reward, taking delight in false humility and worship of angels, intruding into those things which he has not seen, vainly puffed up by his fleshly mind, and not holding fast to the Head, from whom all the body,

95

nourished and knit together by joints and ligaments, grows
with the increase that is from God.

Colossians 2:18–19

The Bible never says for believers not to talk to angels
or interact with them. It warns us not to worship them. If
I have a conversation with you over a cup of tea, it doesn't
mean I am worshiping you! If we team up on a project and
we are working together, again, truly, I am not worshiping
you. I promise.

Scriptures are filled with angelic visitations and interac-
tions. Early Church history is packed with encounters with
the angelic. It is clear from the book of Acts that the early
Church understood how to partner with the full provision of
the supernatural realm for the purposes of God in the earth.

I will be talking more about the role of angels and how to
partner with them as a part of the supernatural life later in
this book when we look at walking like Enoch.

6. Miracles Are Only for Places Like Africa

I will admit it. I am totally and utterly privileged to have
lived most of my adult life among the poorest of the poor
in Asia and Africa.

One dusty morning we loaded up our black four-ton truck
we affectionately call "Midnight Glory" and piled in children,
visitors and sound equipment. We headed out several miles
into the bush.

When we stopped, our vehicle spilled us out into a small village market. One village elder we met was losing his eyesight.

My kids and I gathered around him and began to pray, com-
manding his eyes to open and function properly. We stopped

for him to test it out. A beaming smile spread across his face. He could see perfectly.

Another woman observed this and came forward for prayer for her eyes. So we asked the village elder who had just gotten healed to pray for her. She, too, got healed. The whole crowd rejoiced at the goodness of God.

I tell stories of God faithfully bringing His kingdom when I travel and often I hear, "Yes, that's awesome, but you live in Africa."

As if—God works in Africa but not anywhere else. Hello? That is not what you believe, is it? Somehow the enemy has sucker punched the Church in many areas into believing that the realms of the supernatural are primarily for missionaries in the bush of far-flung nations.

If he can trick you into believing, "Well, of course miracles happen there—it's Africa," he will soon have you believing the inverse: that miracles do not happen in the West. And that, my sweet friend, is absolutely not true. Unless you allow it to be.

I have seen food multiply. I have been trans-relocated (like Philip in the book of Acts). I have seen healings in America as well as in Africa and Asia. I can just as easily step into the realm of God's kingdom in Europe or the U.S. as I can in Uganda or Uzbekistan. God is not bound by geography, but He does often allow Himself to be limited by our belief systems. If we believe miracles are only for Africa, we just might have to go there to see them.

But if we allow Him to transform us by the making new of our mindsets—literally changing the way we think and understand our world so that we are surrendered to Him—then the supernatural life we are created for will begin opening up all around us, regardless of our address.

7. The Supernatural Is Always Extraordinary

Is it?

I was barely twenty years old. I spent the last months of my teenage years somewhere in the rainy season mud of rural Bangladesh. I was thousands of miles from anything remotely familiar, deposited as a wide-eyed teenager four miles past the middle of nowhere. I was utterly convinced that I had found the ends of the earth.

It was a land of ox carts and rickshaws, spices and silk rainbows. And I was as green to it all as the new growth stretching as far as my eye could see in the liquid fields of rice around me.

It was my first introduction to the raw truth that burns deeply. Miles do not a missionary make. All my flaws and weaknesses and needs for grace were only magnified there. They had not miraculously disappeared somewhere over the Atlantic and Indian Oceans.

At first I failed desperately. Each dawn came with new lessons in loving more deeply than language and laying down my right even to have an opinion. It was a beautiful, excruciating season of growth.

I needed to learn that sometimes the supernatural comes in very ordinary ways.

One evening a knock came at my door as shadows stretched long across the floor. I was in my room longing for something, anything, familiar.

It was our sweet Saroti—a little, round woman who served far more than our meals and cooked far more than food. She loved me. My first attempt at tying my own sari almost caused her to roll with laughter. With one tug she twirled me out of six yards of fabric and retied a proper outfit for me to wear.

She slipped into my room bearing biscuits and spiced tea. Her smile lit up the dim corners. I began to learn through her that evening that some of God's greatest gifts are quiet surprises.

Can supernatural encounters come in worn tin cups of tea? Can Communion be offered by cracked hands, roughened from years of tilling fields, washing clothes and cleaning floors? Can Communion in its truest sense be offered at all with hands yet unbroken?

She broke the cookie-like wafer and offered me broken bread. I paused. These same hands had buried babies deep in the earth. She poured out sweetness and spice. She who had poured out her heart in pain and loss and grief bent low to love me. I was humbled by truth. She looked at me, light dancing in her eyes. I took the cup she offered and drank it with the deepest gratitude for God's compassion and answer to my prayer.

Supernatural moments are not always the most extraordinary ones. Some days they are wrapped in simplicity, hidden in swaddling clothes and born in unexpected places.

We just have to have eyes to see them.

8. "Supernatural Gifting" Means You Are Supposed to Be in Vocational Ministry

We are not all called to vocational ministry. Our gifts will indeed make room for us, but just because someone can move in healing or see prophetically does not necessarily mean he or she is called to exercise these gifts in the sphere of ministry as a full-time occupation.

There seems to be a default button in some parts of the church that says the highest aspiration in the Christian life is to be in full-time vocational ministry. Jesus talked about this. Well, in a roundabout way. To me, it is one of the most sobering things He ever said.

> "Many will say to Me in that day, 'Lord, Lord, have we not prophesied in Your name, cast out demons in Your name, and done many wonders in Your name?' And then I will declare to them, 'I never knew you; depart from Me, you who practice lawlessness!'"
>
> Matthew 7:22–23

This passage was not directed at the unbelieving world, but at those who were believers, even those who were walking in some awesome giftings. Hmmm. Eeek. You mean gifts are not proof of being on the right track? Uh-oh.

No, supernatural gifts do not earn brownie points or impress God. They are gifts. I am grateful for all the gifts He gives and eagerly pursue more. But it is all about relationship and intimacy with Him, not performing for Him.

Depart from Me. I never knew you. I never had close intimate fellowship with you. Wow.

You who practice lawlessness. Now wait just a minute. How can prophesying, casting out demons and doing wonders in Your name be *lawlessness*, Jesus?

Have you ever wondered that? Me too. So I looked deeper.

While the New Testament manuscripts we have were written in Greek, the world in which Jesus lived and moved was largely Hebraic in its culture and understanding. So, aspiring Berean that I am, I want to look at what *they* understood Him to say in *their* context so I can see what He was getting at. That means looking at the Hebrew concepts, not the Greek ones.

I am so grateful for my ancient Hebrew classes now and even my classes that taught me about being a Berean. They really have been useful!

Hebrew is an amazing language. Its very letters are actually pictures with layers of meaning that tell stories based on how they were combined. The letters in the word *avon*—which means "lawlessness" or "iniquity"—are the *ain*, the *vav* and the *nun*. Put them together and the story they tell translates as: *Whatever the eye hooks into, multiplies.*

In other words, whatever captivates your focus is what multiplies in your life.

So what I gather Jesus was saying is if we start doing something good, even something supernatural, just because it looks good on someone else, but it is not flowing out of a place of our own intimacy and relationship with Him, it is nothing but trouble.

We are not going to come before Him one day and be rewarded for how miraculous our ministries were or how big they became. We will be measured by that which He has written out in our destiny scroll before one word of it came to be.

> For we are His workmanship, created in Christ Jesus for good works, which God prepared beforehand that we should walk in them.
>
> Ephesians 2:10

Here is my question, then: Out of the place of intimacy with Jesus, are we walking in the fullness of the supernatural provision of God for what He has called us to become and do? Or are we trying to do what looks good on someone else?

We are all in full-time ministry, no matter what our vocation is. One of the most prophetic people I know in the earth today happens to be a businessman. I celebrate the gifts and callings of others, but I desire just one thing: to walk fully in the mandate of heaven over my life and none other.

A hurting, hungry world is desperate for answers that transcend their natural circumstances. And Jesus has one Body on the earth right now to deliver them. Us.

9. If I Can Get Just One More Impartation

In case you don't have this word in your vernacular, here is a quick definition of *impartation*: God transferring a supernatural reality into your life from another person's life or from a corporate setting where He is moving.

Let me start by saying, I love impartation. I believe in it with all my heart. If God is moving powerfully in a place, I will fly across continents to receive from what He is pouring out. It is awesome, right, good and holy, and I am not downplaying it in any way. I honor the dynamics of impartation and regularly seek to place myself in positions to receive more from heaven.

But sometimes a little sneaky thought tries ever so hard to creep into my thought patterns: *If I can just get one more impartation, I will have what I need.*

I know this is a myth because I have had to deal with it in my own journey. And I know by experience that if I fall into its clutches, it can send me on an endless merry-go-round of chasing meeting after meeting, only to leave disappointed. Been there. Done that. Have some T-shirts.

Some of the deepest God encounters I have experienced thus far have been alone at home. The greatest impartations I have received have usually come through relationship. Or they have come directly from Jesus in those places of encounter or in corporate settings of worship and ministry.

Some things in the kingdom can be imparted, but many, many must be cultivated. And there are two things that I know I absolutely cannot in any way successfully impart:

1. I cannot give away what I do not have or impart that which is not a part of me.
2. I cannot impart to you my secret history with God.

If I cannot give these things to someone else, then no one else can give them to me. That means I have to go after them and pursue them for myself.

I have had people ask me to impart all I carry to them. And I tell you I really do not think they would like that . . . unless they would like me to impart all the heartache, all the breaking, all the dying and all of the cost to carry the call.

The question, dear reader, is *How much do you want? How hungry are you?* Sometimes Papa wants us to walk in what He has given, even while we eagerly set our desire for more of Him.

I am so hungry for Him that I am willing to receive His impartation through any vessel at any time in any place by any means He so chooses. But I also know that no one can walk out my journey with Jesus for me.

There are things I need to receive through impartation, but there are many more that must be grown through cultivation in the context of my daily walk with Him.

10. Bells, Whistles and Tap-Dancing Angels

Tap-dancing angels. Who could resist those, right?

Oh, we do live in a culture of comparison, don't we? Bigger is always better. I have fallen so often into the trap of thinking that the big, amazing ways God comes are somehow more important than the quiet small ways. But that is not so at all.

There is nothing wrong with desiring deeper levels of experience with Jesus. That is called hunger. We need to be hungry. It is what propels us onward in our journeys with Him.

There is even something called holy jealousy. When I hear someone has experienced something more from Jesus than I have in an area, often it provokes me to go deeper with Him myself. That is all good and right.

The problem comes when we start comparing notes and measuring ourselves by others. Having bells, whistles and tap-dancing angels in my supernatural experiences does not make me mature, more anointed or more loved. It just means I have had bells, whistles and tap-dancing angels in my experiences.

Your level of maturity is not necessarily synonymous with the level or types of supernatural experiences you have had. It is what you do with those experiences that counts. One type of revelation is not necessarily more significant than another. The question, again, is not how you received the revelation, but what you are doing with what you have received.

Practical Keys: Slaying Myths and Monsters

Wow. Those are a lot of myths and monsters. And this is certainly not an exhaustive list, not by any means.

Do any of the ones I mentioned sound even remotely familiar to you?

Just in case one or two might resemble something you, too, have walked through, I want to take a moment to talk about how to slay a myth, how to kill a monster lie.

A lie has power only in the darkness. It is pretty simple to stop those things dead in their tracks. This is a big part of the renewing of our minds Romans 12:1–2 talks about and stepping into receiving the fullness of what Jesus has accomplished for us on the cross.

The hardest part in dealing with a lie is often seeing that it is there. We really need the Holy Spirit to show us even what operates in our own hearts! Once you know it is there, the work begins.

Simply come into God's presence by faith. *Father, I enter Your presence by faith*. Recognize the lie. *This right here is a big, dumb lie*. Bring it into the light of the truth of who God is. *Papa, I come before You with this lie*. Take responsibility for it. *I have believed this lie*. Ask forgiveness. *I am sorry for believing this lie. Please forgive me*. Receive His forgiveness. *Thank You for forgiving me!* Trade the lie and all the power it held in for truth and freedom in Jesus. *Jesus, I give this lie to You [name it] and I receive the truth of who You are in its place that says [the opposite of the lie] and sets me free!*

So shall we give this a whirl?

May I pray for you?

Precious Jesus, I ask right now that You would swoop down with Your tangible presence and surround my friend who is reading this right now. I thank You that You silence any and every whisper of condemnation with Your love. I thank You that Your beautiful light shines on any area where my friend feels trapped by the cage of one of these myths. I ask, Jesus, that You would come, unlock the door and set him, set her free to fly into the heights of Your grace and the depths of Your love. Thank You, Jesus. Amen.

Discussion Questions and Activation Exercise

- What premise do you tend to discern things by? Do you generally look to prove something wrong or to prove it right? Ask Jesus what it means for you to be a Berean.
- Which of the ten myths could you readily identify operating in your own journey?
- Pick one myth you identified and begin to process with Jesus how believing that myth has impacted your journey. Don't just think about it. Talk with Jesus about it and ask Him to show you.
- Is there a myth you disagree with? Practice being a Berean and examine the Scripture daily to try and prove it right. Feel free to disagree if you come to a different conclusion.

Activation: Pick one of the myths you identified as having had an impact on you. Come into the presence of the Lord. Spend some time with Him, and practice the process of exchange mentioned above. Spend more time soaking in the truth like a sponge. Use what you have learned so far not just to agree with it intellectually but to actively experience the truth in Jesus.

5

Growing in the Supernatural

It is 2001. I am living in South Asia.

After a year of every plan I had falling apart in front of me, I am staring blankly at the walls. I am so tired. Soon I will be on a plane back for a few weeks to visit the U.S.A. I am counting hours, not days. Melting in India's pre-monsoon heat, the hot wet air is a sauna from which I cannot escape.

My things are in storage. In a few days I am scheduled to minister at a youth conference. But I have nothing to give. Tired, hot, empty, frustrated, hungry and desperate for more of Jesus, I nestle into a booth in a closet-sized restaurant in the backpacker district of the city.

Cool drink in hand, I purposefully ignore the din around me and immerse myself in the one book I have with me that is still unread: *The Fire of His Holiness* by Sergio Scataglini.

I get halfway through the first chapter. Sergio describes a time when God encounters him so powerfully that he has to crawl up the stairs. This desperate cry rises from my own belly, and hot tears begin to stream down my face. I want *that*. I want His fire.

An intense longing hits my heart so hard it is physically painful. I excuse myself from staying at my sweet friends' home and check myself into a small hotel where I can seek God in private. I have five days until the conference. I bring five gallons of drinking water with me and lock the door.

Raw hunger that hurts and aches and stirs within lays me low each day on my face. My nose to carpet, I inhale carpet fibers. I want an encounter with His fire. I want to be consumed and changed. I cannot go back and I cannot go on until I meet Him in the fire of who He is.

One day, two days, three days I keep pressing in. Jesus is speaking and taking me through Scripture, but I feel absolutely nothing. Four days, five days go by very quietly with no burning hot, shaking demonstration of His manifest presence.

It feels as if nothing happened. I fight off deep disappointment.

All that I feel is not all that is real. I know this. And I leave these five days with a whispered promise: "Beloved, the days of dignity for you are over, but the days of demonstration are just beginning."

Now, when Jesus tells you something like this, you have to wonder what exactly He means. Honestly, I feel no different, but I choose to trust in what I cannot see.

I step into the youth conference that, truthfully, I do not even want to be at. The first three days are tough plowing. Speakers are ignored. Worship is mocked, and kids are trying to make out in the back pews during the sessions. It is pure chaos.

But on the fourth day everything changes. The speaker stands up to speak, and I watch the atmosphere shift. Muffled sobs begin erupting throughout the room as the tangible fear of the Lord begins to move. Shortly afterward, young people from all over the room are weeping and running to the front of the room to fall on their faces and cry out for God.

Our team gathers around them praying. I join in to pray for those who have come forward. One by one they start to scream and shake, saying they are being burned by fire. Finally, I take the microphone and explain the fire of God that is falling so they can understand what is happening to them.

Here I am, watching what I prayed for personally happen all around me. The lives of these young people are being changed. We are in the middle of a full-blown visitation of God's fire. But I still personally feel absolutely nothing.

Then I hear Jesus chuckle right in the middle of it all. "See, beloved, take heart. Just because you don't feel anything doesn't mean nothing is happening. Sometimes you have to go with what you *know*, not what you feel."

I hear His words and realization hits. I had stepped into that hotel room with a determination in my heart to not move until something happened. Five days later, something had very definitely happened inside of me, even if it was not the way I was expecting. Now I am watching, amazed as His grace is released to others around me. Truly all that I feel is not all that is real.

Have You Ever Felt Stuck?

The Lord's invitation into the supernatural life is a summons to grow deeper, go lower and stay closer. It truly is all about the journey. And all journeys that matter start deep inside of us.

Have you, dear reader, ever felt stuck in your journey with God as if you are just about to step into a deeper level with Him, and you cannot quite get there? And then there are those infuriating seasons when it feels more like two steps forward and three steps back. Ever had one of those?

I sure have. "Growing pains" are normal. Take a deep breath and say with me, "I am normal." You are not a second-class child of the King because you occasionally hit a learning curve. It is only evidence that you are growing. And that is a very good thing!

I am not talking about what the historical Christian mystic writers dubbed the *dark night of the soul*. Or what some call a *wilderness season*. We will talk about that experience in the next chapter. Here I am just talking about the everyday ruts that we sometimes get our feet stuck in on the journey into Jesus, and how we can pull out of them.

Then there is the learning curve that comes when God starts speaking to us and showing us things. What do we do with what we receive? And how do we position ourselves to receive more?

Do you remember in the beginning of this book I mentioned that our ultimate invitation into the supernatural life is the Father, Son and Holy Spirit sharing themselves with us and transforming us to look like them?

The goal of God meetings and encounters is not merely the experiences themselves but our growing up into maturity and intimacy in Him and being able to bring what we encounter in heaven back with us to change the earth. But wouldn't it be nice to have someone share a few pointers on what to do when we hit bumps in the road and how to keep moving forward? Here are some thoughts from my journey.

Trust His Faithfulness

Okay, Jesus. So living a supernatural life is totally and completely dependent on Your faithfulness, not necessarily what I feel. And You are faithful. Regardless. I get it.

The Lord knows I can be a bit relentless. When I see something more in Him, I go after it with all I am. I wanted to understand about His fire. So I began to study every time fire of any kind was mentioned in Scripture to help me get a fuller picture.

What got me going is a principle in the kingdom called the "law of first mention." Basically this principle says that the first time a topic is introduced in Scripture it lays foundational implications for the way it is understood in context throughout the rest of Scripture. In other words, when anything appears in the Bible for the first time, we should pay special attention to it.

And here is what I learned: The first time fire of any kind is mentioned in the Bible is in the context of God making a covenant with Abram in Genesis 15. In Genesis 12 Abram heard God say: "Leave all that you have known, all that is safe and familiar, and follow Me to a land I will show you."

To truly understand how radical this is, it helps to have a bit of context. Abram did not have the advantage of five thousand years of biblical history to reveal who God was to him. This was no nice little spiritual exercise. Can you imagine? The God of the universe calls you out of all you have ever known at age 75 with the promise of becoming a great nation when you don't even have your first child. How's that for an encounter that shakes things up a bit?

I can imagine the responses of his friends. "Abram, man, you are nuts. You don't even have kids. And now you are going to follow this God you don't know to a land that you have never seen to become the father of a nation when you are still childless, you're 75 and your servant is your heir? Yeah, good one, man. What were you drinking last night?"

It is not surprising that three chapters and some years later we find Abram asking some questions when nothing has visibly changed. Remember, questions are good as long as we know where to hang them.

God takes him outside and shows him the stars and tells him his descendants shall be as numerous as those stars. Abram believes God. Okay, that astounds me. Seriously. Way to go, Abram!

He asks, "God, how do I know I will possess the land You promised?"

God responds by making a covenant. Abram, like the rest of the ancient world, understood covenants. It was a binding agreement—a legal document, like a contract.

But covenant-making was not a neat, tidy process of signing on the dotted line. It was a bloody, messy affair. An animal would be cut in half and the agreement was ratified as both parties walked between each half of the carcass, saying, in effect, "So may it be done to me if I break my agreement."

In this case God asks Abram to bring five animals and cut each of them in two. I imagine this took all day. It is hard enough work to cut a goat in half, let alone a cow. It takes my boys hours to slaughter and butcher just one goat for special occasion meals in Sudan.

Well, as the sun is setting, a deep sleep—more accurately understood as a trance—comes on Abram. He does not just nod off and fall asleep. The presence of God comes on him in such a way that he enters a visitation that renders him unaware of everything but God.

In this encounter, God appears as a flaming torch and a smoking oven to pass through the pieces of the animals. God alone ratifies the covenant. Abram never walks through the pieces of the animals.

How much more can we, who live this side of the cross, trust His faithfulness? The supernatural life is rooted and grounded in the Lord's complete trustworthiness, regardless of our current experience.

In other words, just because I have not personally seen a dead person raised does not mean God has stopped raising the dead or that His promise is not for me. God walks through the pieces twice, saying that this promise depends on His faithfulness alone. In this supernatural journey, if I want to walk in the fullness of every promise He has given, I must never reduce my theology or my expectation to the level of my current experience.

My face is set toward Him. God is who He says, and He does what He promises. Period. Just look at Abram.

Don't Try Too Hard

And here is another thought from my journey that may help you: When you hit a bump in the road, keep moving forward.

As I said, I have always been an all-or-nothing kind of girl. It is just how I am wired. If I go after something, it is full speed ahead. God likes that about me. He really does. But sometimes my natural wiring would get me into trouble were it not for a whole lot of His amazing grace.

When I run ahead and make things too complicated, He says with a smile, "Whoa, there, sweetheart. Just stop a minute and take a deep breath. You are trying *way* too hard. You don't have to figure it out."

It is a bit like learning to ride a bike. Now, having just one leg, I have never learned how to ride a bike. But I have watched enough of my kids in Sudan go through the process to gather a few things.

For example, they learn how to balance and pedal on rough, unpaved trails. I watch them take off. They do just fine until they realize they are riding on their own and that staying upright is up to them. The harder they try to keep vertical, the more they tense up. The more they tense up, the harder it is to balance, and the closer they get to a scraped knee. But if they simply let the bike work for them, relax and lean into the bumps, suddenly they are flying over our village paths!

Sometimes when I feel the edges of something more from Jesus around me but I cannot quite seem to step into it, I am simply trying too hard to stay vertical.

This invitation into the supernatural life is an invitation of pure grace.

Jesus has already done it all. All we have to do is lean in to what He has done. We position ourselves for His promise by our desire. But even that desire is a gift from Him! He gives us the desires of our heart as we delight in Him (see Psalm 37:4). It truly is all grace.

I am humbled, relieved and set free by this. I don't have to figure it out. I don't have to make it happen. I can stop trying so hard, take a deep breath and know.

Be still, and know that I am God; I will be exalted among
the nations, I will be exalted in the earth!

Psalm 46:10

I Had an Encounter: Now What Do I Do?

What about when you have a vision, a dream or an encounter
in God's tangible presence—what happens then? For me,
personally, one of the biggest learning curves has come in
learning what to do with such an experience.

So you have a mind-blowing, life-changing, amazing encounter with God. What do you do next? Post it on Facebook?
Blog it? Submit it to a prophetic email listserv for publication? Set up a meeting with your pastor with a warning as
to where he or she may be missing it? All these are tempting
options, but there are a few things to consider before choosing one of them.

One of the most crucial things about receiving revelation
is knowing what and what *not* to do with it.

Recommended Things to Do:

- Journal it or record it somewhere safe. Date it and write
  it down as best you can remember it.
- Talk more with Jesus about it. Realize that many visions,
  like dreams, are filled with symbols that are not always
  to be understood literally.
- Ask the Holy Spirit to give you more understanding from
  the Scriptures concerning what the encounter means.
  Ask Him to help you make sure it lines up with the
  character and ways of God.

- Ponder it in your heart. Don't rush into interpreting what it means or how it should be applied. Most prophetic mistakes come not in receiving the revelation but in wrongly interpreting and applying it.
- If it is a vision, spend time remembering it and asking God to show you more.
- Ask Jesus for wisdom in what He wants you to do with the revelation. Some things are for saying; many more are for praying. All actions should be measured by the boundaries of His love.
- Share it humbly with leaders you are in relationship with, and invite them to speak into it (especially if you feel it has a corporate application). Ask them to pray about it.

Things Recommended Not to Do:

- Assume you know the interpretation or application automatically.
- Embellish it so it sounds more spiritual.
- Post it all over Facebook or blog it online—until you have processed it with Jesus thoroughly and know what He is asking of you in it, and if it is ready to be shared. I have had to learn the hard way that any word He brings through my life in power, He first works into my life. For a revelation to have spiritual authority, it must be made real in us first.
- Make something happen. Don't act on any revelation contrary to who God is in His character as revealed in Scripture or in a way that is condemning or unloving. "But the wisdom that is from above is first pure, then

peaceable, gentle, willing to yield, full of mercy and good fruits, without partiality and without hypocrisy" (James 3:17).

- Expect that any major correctional or directional word will be received well without the context of an established relationship in which you have been given authority to speak into it in such a way.

- Sit your leadership down to straighten them out based on your new revelation. That is spiritual manipulation, which is, as I said in the last chapter, witchcraft. Witchcraft is not found only in occult circles cloaked with long, pointy hats and brooms. Any time we engage in control or try to manipulate the outcome of things is basically witchcraft. It happens every day in church. Simply rest, knowing that if God is asking you to share something with your leaders and you have done so in love, honor and humility, then what they do with it is their responsibility alone before God.

Treasure Your Pearls

I have had to learn some lessons the hard way. I have had to learn others the *very* hard way. I am so glad Papa redeems time and learning curves. He picks us up and brushes us off and says, "Come on, let's try again, honey!"

This book is all about the invitation to journey deeper into His heart and engage the supernatural reality we are created for. And the lesson I am about to share has been a messy, crucial one that I am still growing in on this journey. Let's just say I am learning to live in the balance between the love that always trusts and the wisdom that guards her pearls and ponders them in her heart until the right time for them to be displayed.

Here is some really good advice from Jesus:

> "Do not give what is holy to dogs, and do not throw your pearls before swine, or they will trample them under their feet, and turn and tear you to pieces."
>
> Matthew 7:6, NASB

I always thought this referred to people you don't know, or people you know are not "safe," or people who are outside the kingdom. I missed the point entirely. This has been one of the lessons I have had to learn the very hard way.

It has taken me years to begin to learn that all I see is not all I should say. Just because I see it does not mean I should share it!

Sometimes, out of the sheer excitement of glimpsing more of the beauty of God, I have innocently let others play with my pearls. At other times I have intentionally traded them in trying to prove myself. It often goes something like this:

Me: Wow, God's been doing so much lately. (That is, please ask me what so I can show off a pearl or two.)

Someone else: Really? Do tell.

Me: Well, yesterday I was working on administration, and His presence came so strongly.

Someone else: Yeah, that happens to me a lot. So what did He show you? (Slam! So let me see your pearls. Show me what you've got.)

Me: I saw this vision of Jesus blowing up boxes. And He said, "I will not be confined or contained by systems of men in the coming days."

118

Someone else: Oh, I've seen that, too—last year. You are
finally catching up. Good job. (I'll take that pearl, thank
you. Oops, there it goes into the mud of my insecurity.
Now let me cut you down to size so I feel better.)

Okay, so tell me, where did I go wrong? How about caving
in to temptation the minute my heart felt pressured to prove
something, or setting myself up to be asked so I can have a
platform to share? I should have graciously backed off with a
nebulous "Oh, a few things I'm still processing. Love learning
more from Him. So what's up in your world?"

Often we unintentionally trade revelation or encounters
God gives us as if they're Monopoly money to purchase what
feels like more secure spiritual real estate. Then, when someone comes along with a revelation that feels greater than ours,
we feel our security threatened.

If someone comes along with a deeper understanding than
I have and I feel threatened by that one little bit, it is a big sign
that my identity is misplaced, and I am in danger of trading
in my pearls for a false sense of security.

Our security should be based on being His, on being secure in His love, and not from the revelations or experiences
we have of Him. Security based in love never has anything
to prove.

When I looked at Matthew 7:6 more closely, I realized it
is basically saying that we should not give what is set apart
or sacred to those who will not understand it or value it for
what it is. Dogs have no reference point for something being
sacred. And swine, if left to themselves, will eat anything and
stay for weeks rolling in their own filth. So do not throw your
pearls (those precious bits of revelation and things Jesus has

119

given) before those who choose to stay in the muck of their own issues because they will trample your pearls beneath those issues and then turn and tear you to pieces.

Jesus is simply talking about discernment and healthy boundaries for what we do with revelation—the good things our Father in heaven gives us when we ask Him. He recommends boundaries that bring life and allow love to function and flow to its full extent. Not boundaries based in fear, but those erected in grace and true wisdom.

One too many times I have traded my pearls in to try to prove my own spirituality in hopes of getting noticed or maintaining my spiritual real estate. I have had to repent big-time.

There have been times I felt I didn't just lose a few pearls to the muck, but I had my face planted in it. As much as I wanted to point to other people's issues, the real truth was I had unknowingly tried to use the pearls I had been given by Papa to prove my identity and demonstrate how spiritual I was.

I was not treasuring my pearls; I was unintentionally trading them in under pressure, pawning them off to the highest bidder.

During one such time, I was weeping facedown in worship. Suddenly I had a vision. Jesus walked up to me and started picking up my pearls that were lost in the muck and mire. He knew just where they were and washed them off gently, collecting them quietly in His hand.

I wiped tears from my eyes and watched Him string them into the most beautiful pearl necklace that I have ever seen. He then placed this necklace on my neck. I wept at His tender grace that would fully restore what I had given away.

So what about you, dear reader? Have you lost some pearls in the mud of issues? Jesus knows just where they are. And He has already paid the price for their restoration.

Hold On to the Promise

Have you ever planted a seed? Even a seed in the best soil does not become a plant overnight. Growth takes time. At times it even takes tenacity.

Each encounter we have with God's presence, each new understanding from Scripture, every vision from heaven, every revelation from the heart of Jesus—all these are seeds planted in the soil of our hearts that God wants to grow into a garden of fruitfulness.

> "But the ones that fell on the good ground are those who, having heard the word with a noble and good heart, keep it and bear fruit with patience."
>
> Luke 8:15

As we spend time with Jesus every day, He makes the soil of our hearts fertile places for revelation to grow.

It is so interesting to me that for our lives to be considered "good ground," we have to keep the seed and bear fruit with patience. Our work is not just a passive receiving but an active engaging.

The word used for "keep" can also be translated "hold it fast, keep it secure, set and hold one's course, guard with a military posture, protect, be pregnant (hold until the time of birth)." Bearing fruit with patience also speaks of endurance, perseverance and standing one's ground.

Walking in the supernatural realms of God's kingdom is

not just about supernatural experiences and gifting, then. It is also about the tenacity to hold onto His promises for ten, fifteen, twenty, thirty years or more, if need be. Rarely do things happen overnight. I am just now stepping into things I saw ten and fifteen years ago. What God works through us, He first works in us.

> These all died in faith, not having received the promises, but having seen them afar off were assured of them, embraced them and confessed that they were strangers and pilgrims on the earth.
>
> Hebrews 11:13

Some of the greatest men and women of God in the Bible did not fully receive the things they saw in the kingdom manifest in their day, even though they embraced them fully in the supernatural realms of God's promise. They did not give up. Ever. They possessed the promise by faith and did not let go, even though they did not see it come to pass. And that is considered success. That, too, is supernatural.

I want to be like them when I grow up.

This life we live is one lived by faith. We are called to walk in the unseen and from there to change the world we see around us. So whatever you do, hold on to the promise. And you will find one day that the Promise is holding on to you.

Practical Keys: Honoring What You Have

One of the biggest keys I have found to growing in the supernatural is the key of honor. What you honor multiplies in your life. If you want more of God's supernatural kingdom realm of revelation moving and operating around you, learn to honor what He has already given.

If you don't feel that you have much yet, ask God to show you how, when and where He has already moved in your life. Sometimes we realize what He is doing only after the fact. Honor it with thanksgiving. Don't wait for the big whammy from heaven. Honor the smallest and faintest whispers from His heart to yours. Here are two practical ways to honor what God is giving you and thus make room for more:

1. Record the Vision: Keep a Journal

I know you may not be a writer. But don't consider keeping a journal a literary exercise. It is simply practice in remembering and thus honoring what God gives. Our words frame our worlds. Journaling does not have to happen in a flowery notebook or even in complete sentences. There are as many ways to journal as there are people who keep them.

Here are a few ways to journal:

- Encounter journal: a place to record visions, experiences with God, how He is moving, what He is saying, what you see.
- Dream journal: a place to record your dreams or revelations in the night that often fade off and disappear in the first five or ten minutes of waking up.
- Visual/creative journal: pictures, phrases, colors, symbols . . . creatively engaging with what God is showing you.
- On your handheld: perfect for those of us on the go who don't want to haul notebooks across continents but who also don't want to forget what God is showing us.

- On your computer in a separate file: I will often grab Internet images that speak to me about what God is showing me for personal use in my prayer times. (Also, if you want to carry your journal history with you but don't want to type up ten years of revelation, I have started taking a digital camera and photographing each page of my journal when it is finished and putting those photos in a dated folder on my computer.)
- Study journal: what God is showing you in the Scripture and through understanding of the revelations given. You could say these are your Berean notes.
- All in one: a creative collection of any and all of the above! I am not super-organized, so in some seasons of my life I simply toss it all into one book.

2. Remember to Focus

As I have said before and will say again: What we focus on, we empower.

If you want to grow in an area, spend proactive time in your day engaging that area. Walking in the supernatural with Jesus is something you have to pursue as a priority and actively engage, not just passively receive.

> And you will seek Me and find Me, when you search for Me with all your heart.
>
> Jeremiah 29:13

A more literal reading of Jeremiah 29:13 says we will search God out and desire Him and He will come forth so that we find Him, when we follow in pursuit of Him with all our hearts.

No one can build my secret history with God for me. The level of intimacy I walk with Him in is a direct function of my hunger and desire. I can have as much of Him and His kingdom as I want. The question is: How much do I want? How hungry am I? If you are not that hungry, ask Him to put hunger in you.

One of the best ways I know to get back in touch with my hunger when I have gotten too externally focused is by spending some time fasting. I don't fast to twist God's arm or get Him to do something. I don't fast because it earns me brownie points in heaven or increases my spirituality. I don't fast religiously or with a strict set of rules.

I fast because I want to be in touch with my need for Him on every level, and I want the feeling of physical hunger to put me back in touch with my spiritual need. Often during those times of fasting, I feel nothing. But as I shared earlier in this chapter about what happened in India, breakthrough often happens on its heels.

When we focus on something, we empower it to operate. What we desire, we create a platform for. Again, the question is not so much how God is showing me His heart, but what I am doing with what He has shown me.

No matter how faint a whisper is from Him, it is still Him. Lean in. Thank Him for speaking. Ask questions about it. Build relational history. Spend time in His presence getting to know what He looks and sounds like.

May I pray for you?

Father, I ask that You would continue to stir hunger inside the one reading these words right now. I ask that You would awaken sleeping promises You have given this dear one, even from decades ago. Let disappointment and hope deferred fall away in the light of Your utter faithfulness.

Every promise from You is Yes and Amen through the anointing of Your Son, Jesus. Let us see, be persuaded and fully embrace every promise You have for us to walk in as Your children, that Your kingdom may come in and through us on the earth. Amen.

Discussion Questions and Activation Exercise

- Are you feeling as if little or nothing is happening in your journey with Jesus? Can you take a closer look and see more clearly what is being accomplished? Ask Jesus to show you.

- What are ways you know God has communicated with you in the past that you can celebrate now in the present? Things like His still, small voice, through the Scriptures, in visions, in dreams, in trances (the overcoming of your senses), through nature and in metaphors—to name a few possibilities.

- Have you ever been trying too hard in an area with God? Are you trying too hard now? Ask Jesus what He wants to say about that.

- Have you ever exchanged your pearls for conveying spirituality or receiving a sense of security? Maybe take a moment now and talk to Jesus about that. And ask Him to get those pearls back.

- What promises are you holding on to no matter what? What does this mean to you? Take some time and ask

Jesus to take you back into the promises He has given you and increase the expectation of them in your heart.

Activation: Take one of the ways God has spoken to you in the past, one of the experiences He reminds you of, and use it to go deeper. The same way you would use the Scripture as a gateway, go back to this experience and remember what it felt like, what God spoke to you and what you saw. Don't be surprised if you suddenly go deeper into that encounter and receive more from Jesus.

6

When All Goes Silent

I wake to the moist heat of early spring in South Asia, the last scenes of my dream flashing before me in vivid colors. Rubbing sleep from my eyes, I grab a notebook to write the dream so I do not forget.

Two small planes fly into a bank of ominous greenish-black clouds. Winds and torrential rains buffet both planes' every maneuver. The first plane is thrown off course, losing its orientation, and soon falls, spiraling out of the sky. The second plane is tossed about in the violent weather, but it eventually flies through to the other side.

As I wake, I hear the loving voice of Jesus whisper, "Beloved, the bad news is you are entering a stormy season. The good news is you are the second plane. It is time to learn how to fly by your instrument panel."

Flying by Instruments

I did not know how stormy the season would be. Or that from the moment I heard that whisper of His, all would go silent and blank for months and months.

At first, I kept doing what I always did, spending time in stillness waiting to hear His voice. After weeks of static and not much else, I began to feel like God might be knitting on the backside of the universe. Or perhaps I had done something wrong to displease Him.

I went through more weeks of trying to figure it out. Where did I go wrong? No matter how hard I tried to see, it was like I had been expertly blindfolded.

All I could see was my Bible, what God had already promised and what I knew to be true. I tried fasting. I tried rebuking the silence. I tried stomping my foot and having a good old-fashioned tantrum. Nothing relented. (Not that I thought tantrums were the answer. But I was really frustrated. Can you relate at all to feeling like that?) Months dragged by.

Dear reader, do you know how they test instrument-rated pilots? I didn't. I found out much later that they blindfold them to everything *but* their instrument panels in the cockpit of the airplane. The only reference point they have is their understanding of the numbers and gauges on the panel in front of them. And only instrument-rated pilots can fly safely in clouds and storms.

Soon that spring and summer had turned to fall, and I was a student in a five-month training school with an international missions organization in India. It was a growing, stretching time that had almost nothing to do with the classes.

Hidden in my room, I cried myself to sleep almost every night. I felt like I had been plunged into an enormous pitch-black room, and God might be in the room, but He wasn't letting on where He was. I was the one who kept running her hands over the walls looking for the light switch so I could see Him again.

I clung to my journal and Bible. I immersed myself in Scripture even if I didn't feel anything. I began to orient my life based on what God said, who I knew Him to be, based on His promises. The pitch-blackness began to lighten ever so slightly. I could sense His presence if only by sheer faith. I started to know I wasn't alone because He said I wasn't. Not only just because I had an encounter.

Midway through this season, I really did wonder if my sanity was in jeopardy. I begged God to tell me how long this silence would last. In His absolute mercy, He told me that this silent time would end two years from the day I first landed in India. He also gave me one promise. I would come up out of this desert wasteland carried by Him. I cherished those few words as if my life depended on them. In the months ahead, it virtually did.

Part of this discipleship school included an outreach portion. I wound up co-leading our small team. The first half of the outreach went wonderfully, with only normal bumps in the road. But the second half of our time was an unmitigated disaster.

We arrived at our second destination in late January in the middle of near-blizzard conditions. Our hosts had not even prepared the basics for our coming. There was tension from the outset. Our primary host was a local pastor, who had major issues with both women and foreigners. Our sending leadership failed to adequately discern in advance where this pastor was in his understanding. He had been sent an all-Indian team led by two women foreigners. That, my friend, was a recipe for trouble.

In all fairness to him, it was a bad situation that could have been avoided by a little foresight. Hindsight is usually 20/20, isn't it? By the third day this man was responding with violent, erratic behavior, threats to turn us in to the government and death curses. At one point he had me physically pinned against the wall, shouting death threats. We had to pull the team out and make a run for our own safety, only after he stole all our team's money.

I held it together, more or less, until we got all our team members safely put on trains to their respective homes for a break while we sorted the mess out. As soon as they were on their way, my thin façade of normality broke apart. Our host's contorted, rage-filled face kept playing over and over and over again in my head like a broken record. I could feel him grabbing my collar and nearly lifting me off the ground. I could not sleep. I could not eat. I didn't sleep much more than thirty minutes a night for almost the next two weeks.

Soon afterward, because of his ongoing threats to the organization that put on the school, I was put on a plane back to the U.S.A. with less than 24 hours' notice. I was exhausted and deeply shaken by it all.

I arrived back in the U.S. bewildered, emotionally frazzled and possibly with a bit of post-traumatic stress. The dreams I had for India were shattered beyond recognition. All I had to hold on to was the promise of Jesus and His word. He did not rescue me out of that season, but He did walk with me through it.

Almost five months later, I was on my way to move to Colorado to start a new chapter in my life. My routing took me through Kansas City, where I spent several days at the International House of Prayer visiting friends there. My friends were on the night watch, which is like the night shift of worshiping pray-ers who pray through the hours of midnight to six o'clock.

The first two nights I joined them and spent the time reading my Bible and drinking coffee to stay awake. Again I felt and saw nothing except my own raw brokenness. This silent, dark season had been going on for well over a year at that point. The third night I almost stayed home. I had a severe headache. But I felt a very faint tug on my heart that for some reason I needed to be there. So I decided to go, headache and all.

Throughout the night there were calls for those who wanted prayer to raise their hands. I felt so low I did not even want anyone to pray for me. I just wanted to hide. Six in the morning rolled around. And the leaders issued the last call of the night for prayer. One of the first things I heard in months was Jesus saying, "Put your hand up."

"But I don't want to put my hand up."

"Put it up."

"Okay."

A small group of people I had never met gathered round me. I told them I had a headache. They told me I had been called "Beloved by my Father in heaven, and the desert time was over. Now the season changes." They saw me coming up out of the wasteland being carried by Jesus. Remember His promise to me from months before?

I began to weep with the intensity of His love that wrapped around me. These people could have no idea what the words they shared with me meant. Soon the weight of His presence grew so heavy, I could not put words together or sit up without someone holding me in place. It was as if Jesus came and bear-hugged me. I could not walk or talk for over twelve hours. I was carried out of the wasteland in more ways than one.

When this experience began to lift, I realized the date and time. He came not two years to the day I had landed in India, but two years to the *hour* I landed in India, given the time difference. It was as if Jesus had been counting the minutes until He would rush in to engulf me once again in His tangible presence. This season may just have been as hard or harder for Him than it was for me. It still brings tears of gratitude to my eyes even ten years later.

The Preparation of Desperation

Last chapter I promised we would look at a very special and often misunderstood spiritual season sometimes called a *wilderness season* or, in early Christian mystical literature, *the dark night of the soul.*

You, sweet friend, have just read of my first experience of what Saint John of the Cross and other early Church writers call the soul's *dark night.*

What exactly is the dark night of the soul?

It is a time when our experience of God's presence is either cut off completely or is greatly diminished. It is a time we must walk by faith and not by sight. It is a time of very little outward feeling and very little to no dramatic outward encounters. It is often wrought with challenges and difficulty. And all the while it can feel like God is silently knitting on the backside of the universe a few thousand light years away.

Basically, these *dry times* are times of learning how to fly by our instrument panels. And they are some of the most important growing experiences in the supernatural life. They bring the preparation of desperation that creates *in* us a platform for His demonstration *through* us.

There can be a temptation during wilderness times to turn back from God's invitation to come deeper, especially when we don't understand what is happening to us or how to navigate it. If we keep walking onward with God, these seasons will come usually more than once. But they do not have to be discouraging or defeating times. They can become springboards into the deepest places of intimacy we have known yet, if we embrace Jesus within them and allow Him to do His work in our hearts.

The Hiddenness of God

I was in another spiritual dry spell a few years later after settling in Colorado. It was then I heard a teaching by Graham Cooke that forever changed my understanding on the seasons God takes us through as we walk with Him.

Again I was in a time when there was no emotion, no sensation. It was just me holding on because I couldn't let go. Some told me it was burnout and suggested I go out to pasture. I was still in my late twenties so I decided it was a little early to retire.

Others theorized I just needed more soaking prayer. (Also synonymous with waiting prayer, listening prayer or Christian contemplative prayer.) I agreed that was a great idea. But I was a bit perplexed about what to do when *soaking* felt more like *choking* because all tangible experience of the river of God's presence had dried to dust.

In this season, a friend slipped me a copy of Graham Cooke's teaching on seasons of hiddenness and manifestation. Hot tears of gratitude spilled from my eyes as I listened to him unfurl understanding with his lovely British accent right through my iPod, while I curled up in a corner of the Houston airport during a layover. I finally had a name for what was happening to me thanks to his teaching.

I was experiencing a season of hiddenness. Graham's message on this subject was so pivotal because it finally gave me a practical understanding to hold on to that these quiet seasons really were gifts from God to be embraced, not times to just be endured.

In seasons of *hiddenness* God withdraws much of His tangible touch in the arenas of our soul and the physical world in order to draw us deeper into the realm of the spirit. He is not at all absent, regardless of what we feel or don't feel. He is present with us, just interacting in a different way.

Seasons of manifestation are the times He bursts into our realm and is tangibly interacting with us here. But seasons of *hiddenness* are about Him actively drawing us deeper into His realm.

This one insight changed everything.

What about you, friend? Have you, too, had these times when it felt like God was silent and hidden from your sight? What an encouragement to know He is not knitting on the backside of the universe! He is still present with you; He is simply presenting Himself differently.

The seasons of *hiddenness* for me ebb and flow much like the tide. But they have become precious, intimate times when God cements internally in me that which He desires to do externally around me.

They are times of embracing the mystery of not knowing how He will choose to reveal Himself. The hidden seasons test my heart. Can I expect Him but not box Him in with any expectation of how He chooses to come?

They are times of learning to see Him move and enjoy being with Him in new falling snow, in sunsets, as I hear a child's giggle in the airport, as I drink my morning coffee. Times of my faith deepening in the experience of just knowing He is and He is with me regardless of the experience of my faith.

Seasons of hiddenness do not have to be barren times at all. They can be desert places filled with beauty and wonder and burning bushes.

When God withholds the external place of visitation, it is only to build in us an internal place of habitation. This excites me. I want my life to be a place where God doesn't come and go but where He can come and remain.

The Wooing of the Wilderness

"Therefore, behold, I will allure her, will bring her into the wilderness, and speak comfort to her. I will give her her vineyards from there, and the Valley of Achor as a door of hope; she shall sing there, as in the days of her youth, as in the day when she came up from the land of Egypt. And it shall be, in that day," says the LORD, "that you will call Me 'My Husband.'"

Hosea 2:14–16

Another way to describe *the dark night of the soul* or seasons of God's *hiddenness* is as a wilderness time. Wilderness seasons are not all about death as I had once thought; they are actually all about life!

Hosea 2 talks about God's purpose of restoration and deepening of intimacy with Him in the wilderness. In Hosea 2:14–16, God in His love allures and draws His people, walking with them Himself into the desert places. Once there, all that has hindered is stripped away. It is a place where God deals with things that have become idols or distractions to our vision of Him. And in the middle of the most seemingly barren places, God restores our fruitfulness.

It is a kingdom paradox. The valley of *Achor* (which comes from a root word to disturb, to bring trouble, to afflict, literally to roil water) becomes the very entryway into expectancy and hope. In the wilderness, God speaks to the core of who we are. It is a place where we are restored back to our first love.

Immersed in an ongoing, deepening, intimate relationship with Jesus, we are betrothed to Him forever in righteousness and justice, in steadfast love and compassion, in stability and faithfulness. And from this place of intimacy, He opens the heavens and the earth brings forth its harvest.

Wilderness journeys can be profound times that establish our faith and solidify our identity in Him. Sometimes we don't actually need another visitation, vision or revelatory experience. Sometimes we need seasons of walking with Jesus in what He has already given so that it becomes a part of us. These wilderness times are places of learning to live in the reality of His Spirit, not only in our experience of His Spirit's reality.

So, dear reader, how are you finding this? I pray it is as encouraging to you as it has been to me.

It is easy to go to meetings where God is moving powerfully and feel rejected if you are walking through one of these times of *hiddenness*. The whole room may be experiencing the tangible manifestation of God's touch, but if you are in a hidden season, you may feel absolutely nothing.

Been there. I have even ministered praying for people while being in one of these seasons myself. I have seen Jesus profoundly touch the ones I pray for and still I felt absolutely nothing.

It is easy at that point to feel a little like a second-class citizen, a little left out of the party. But the truth is that God is moving every bit as powerfully and deeply regardless of the seeming lack of experience in these times. He is simply moving differently.

His silence does not mean His absence. Neither does it mean His disapproval. Some of God's most precious invitations come wrapped in mystery.

In the times we don't feel His presence, we are having a different type of encounter. Instead of Him encountering us in our realm, Jesus is intent on drawing us into His realm. The quiet times are heaven's invitations to journey deeper.

Jesus in the Wilderness

> Then Jesus, being filled with the Holy Spirit, returned from the Jordan and was led by the Spirit into the wilderness, being tempted for forty days by the devil. And in those days He ate nothing, and afterward, when they had ended, He was hungry.
>
> Luke 4:1–2

A discussion on wilderness seasons would be fairly incomplete without touching on Jesus' own time spent in the wilderness.

The first thing noticeable to me in the accounts of His time there is that the Holy Spirit led Him into the wilderness. Again, it is easy to feel this nebulous sense of condemnation, as if we did something wrong, and the wilderness is like our time-out naughty corner. But, dear one, Jesus had done nothing wrong! He just had heaven open over Him, been affirmed dramatically in public by the Father and was full of the Holy Spirit.

For Jesus, the wilderness was a season of establishing His kingdom in the unseen places. The word *tempted* in this passage is more accurately understood *tested, scrutinized, examined or proven*. For forty days Jesus was tested and examined by the devil and in the end Jesus established His identity by *not* proving Himself.

Let's look at how exactly He was tested, because these areas of testing often come to us, too, in our wilderness times.

Test #1: Provide for Yourself

And the devil said to Him, "If You are the Son of God, command this stone to become bread." But Jesus answered him, saying, "It is written, 'Man shall not live by bread alone, but by every word of God.' "

Luke 4:3–4

Jesus just fasted forty days. Luke says He was famished. It was not as though He somehow floated through that time on a cloud. He physically felt the anguish of a stomach that had been without food for forty days. His body was weak.

The devil came at the exact point of His greatest physical need and said, "Come on, prove Yourself, Jesus. If You are who You say You are, create the provision to meet Your most desperate need. Just make it happen."

The test when we are in the middle of wilderness times can be to make something happen and meet our own felt needs in our own strength instead of trusting God to meet them. We do not ever have to bow to an expectation to just *make* anything happen.

Like Jesus, we do not live by natural bread alone but by every word of God. And for us, Jesus Himself is the Word of God and the bread from heaven we feast on.

Test #2: Possess Power for Yourself

Then the devil, taking Him up on a high mountain, showed Him all the kingdoms of the world in a moment of time. And the devil said to Him, "All this authority I will give You, and their glory; for this has been delivered to me, and I give it to whomever I wish. Therefore, if You will worship before me, all will be Yours."

Luke 4:5–7

The next test came when the devil took Jesus high on a mountain, and showed Him all the kingdoms of the world in a moment of time. This mountain most likely was not a physical mountain, but a spiritual one. Mountains in the Scripture very often speak of high places of governmental authority.

The devil took Jesus to a high place in the spirit and showed Him all of the kingdoms of the earth in an instantaneous snapshot of chronological time. These were the places of authority and government given over by Adam all the way back in the very beginning. That was the only reason the devil had possession of them.

The devil was offering Jesus the power, the authority, the worship that rightly already belonged to Him seemingly without having to pay the price or go through the pain of the journey to legally redeem them. The devil was offering Jesus in effect a shortcut to His destiny. But Jesus understood the only true way to actually buy back what was lost (us) and fulfill the reason He came *was* to pay the price of a journey that had to lead to the cross.

A. W. Tozer once said, "Heresy of method can be just as deadly as heresy of message." A seemingly right result gotten the wrong way in the kingdom of God is not actually a right result. The first test had to do with meeting a physical need. This test, however, was one of Jesus' soul: His mind, will and emotions.

In wilderness seasons, it is so inviting to consider taking shortcuts to our destiny. But there are no shortcuts to intimacy with Jesus. Relationship takes time. Our destiny is not wrapped up in an end result destination. Our destiny is found on the journey with the One who is the Way. And all genuine authority comes out of the place of intimacy with Him. We will be talking more about authority in chapters 8 and 9.

Test #3: Prove Yourself

Then he brought Him to Jerusalem, set Him on the pinnacle of the temple, and said to Him, "If You are the Son of God, throw Yourself down from here. For it is written: 'He shall give His angels charge over you, to keep you,' and, 'In their hands they shall bear you up, lest you dash your foot against a stone.'"

Luke 4:9–11

The last recorded test Jesus walked through in His wilderness trial was wrapped up in the statement, "If You are the

Son of God . . ." It was a challenge to prove the very core of His identity by trying to manipulate God into showing up. The devil even quoted Bible verses to push his case.

When Jesus answered back, "You shall not tempt the Lord your God," I believe He was replying to more than just this most recent challenge. He effectively put the devil back in his place and reminded him of who exactly was God and *who* was not.

When we are in wilderness seasons, it is really tempting to want God to prove Himself to us. To prove that He is really there, that He really cares. And in those moments, we, too, have to rise up and say, "Enough. God is who He says He is. Period. Regardless of what I feel or see right now. He is here. Just because He says He is. I choose trust. And I am not playing this game."

> Now when the devil had ended every temptation, he departed from Him until an opportune time. Then Jesus returned in the power of the Spirit to Galilee, and news of Him went out through all the surrounding region.
>
> Luke 4:13–14

When Jesus returned from this season, He returned in the miraculous, supernatural power of the Spirit. Every area of His being that could have been tested had been tested. And He was shown to be absolutely faithful to His Father in heaven. He was trustworthy to carry the full weight of the demonstration of His Father's desire in the earth.

Wilderness seasons are about God rooting inside us the unshakeable kingdom that He ultimately wants to reveal around us, that we, too, might walk in the full power of His Spirit in this supernatural life.

Practical Keys: How to Walk through the Wilderness

Dear reader, as we have said, these times are vital, necessary seasons. But we are called to walk *through* the wilderness, not buy real estate there. How do we do that without getting stuck in the desert for forty years? How do we walk in such a way that we come up from these times in the power of the Spirit, leaning on Jesus, who is the Lover of our souls (see Song of Solomon 8:5)?

Our hidden life in Jesus is a positional reality that requires a practical outworking in our daily walk with Him. Living supernaturally is first about having our roots planted deep in the unseen bedrock of the character of who God is, regardless of what we feel or see. Our experience of Him is often the fruit that comes from our roots being grounded solidly in Him by faith.

Sensory experience is not the ultimate evidence of the unseen realm; faith is. God Himself is the validation of His promise. A lack of tangible, felt encounter is not a lack of encounter. It is a different kind of encounter. When we are born again into God's kingdom, our spirit man has full access to all Jesus is and has, 24/7. That is truth. Manifestation is one kind of encounter in His kingdom. Faith is another.

Some keys I have found helpful in my own wilderness times with Him:

- Don't panic. Realize you are not alone, regardless of what it feels like.
- Hold on to what God has already promised. Thank Him for it. Press in to gratitude even when you don't feel like it. Find things to be thankful for. Count His smallest gifts.

- Continue to spend time with Him, even if you don't feel anything. Keep making space for His embrace, whether that embrace comes through reading the Bible, holding on to the promise or a tangible encounter.

- Realize the amazing things God is doing in you through this season. Deem it valuable. Rejoice in it. Lean into it. Let it do its full work.

- Don't make any life decisions based on a sensory absence. Hold on to what God has said until He says something different.

- Continue to worship Him and turn your gaze toward Him in faith.

- When the devil's lies try to come—the tests to prove yourself, provide for yourself or take seeming shortcuts do your destiny—make use of "It is written . . ." like Jesus did.

- As crazy as this might sound, if you are in the middle of a dry time, ask Jesus to help you enjoy the season and learn how to fully, completely interact with Him within it so that it fulfills the entire weight of His purpose in your life. The places of our greatest desperation are but the positioning for God's greatest demonstrations to be released in and through our lives.

May I pray for you?

Papa, I ask You right now to show this dear one reading this Your nearness, Your absolute Immanuel, God-with-us presence. In the places You are hidden, restore the adventure of seeking, knowing You are longing to be found. In the places that are dry, I pray that the outrageous beauty of the desert might be seen. I ask the peace of knowing that when sight is cut off, it is a time to learn to fly by what You have already given, so that no cloud, no storm may ever derail Your promise in our lives. Help this amazing friend of mine see all that You are doing in every season of this supernatural journey with You. Amen.

Discussion Questions and Activation Exercise

- When you hear the words *wilderness season*, what images immediately come to mind? Are they ones of barrenness and death or increased intimacy and life? Ask Jesus to re-form those mental images and show you what He sees in the wilderness places.

- Have you ever had a time when you felt like God was "knitting on the backside of the universe"? Can you look back now and see where He was actually very present with you?

- What are some of the "instruments" on your instrument panel God wants you to learn to trust? (Things like His promises to you, Scriptures He has spoken specifically to you, times people have given you prophetic words about your destiny, knowledge of His character, etc.)

- When Jesus was in the wilderness, the devil tried to get Him to take a shortcut to His destiny. Where have you been tempted to take a shortcut to yours? Take those areas it would be tempting to circumvent and turn them into intentional acts of worship to Jesus and places of cultivating intimacy with Him.

- Spend time learning to recognize the ways God shows His nearness and encounters you supernaturally in seemingly ordinary, everyday ways. Write them down, all the quiet ways you are grateful He comes.

Activation: Start a file on your computer or a section in your journal where you keep His promises to you. When the paths of your journey with Him lead through a silent, desert season, go back to them and remember. Know that He is working in you what He desires to release through you. Embrace His grace in the wilderness, and it will lead you into greater fruitfulness than you can imagine.

7

Walking Like Enoch

One evening not long ago, I stand surrounded by smoldering rubbish heaps several hours from my home base in South Sudan. I am visiting friends of mine who live and work in the brothels in one of South Sudan's major cities. Mazes of tin shack lines traverse the smoky squalor as far as I can see. The sun dipping low in the sky, men swagger by in drunken stupors. "Kwaaaaaja [white person], you give me money." Dodging their intoxicated grasps, I pick my way carefully between burning trash mounds and the streams of sewage that carve out their landscape. One thought crosses my mind: *This is a corner of hell crying out for heaven. This is a place crying out for encounter.*

We are invited not only to encounter the realities of heaven but to become God's encounter bringing heaven's realities to the earth.

I look around me, engulfed by a corrugated iron sheet empire built on fear and pain and lust. Women with painted faces lounge in doorways looking for customers, their age-old business booming. They offer themselves for the same price as a box of juice on the streets to pay for their rented tin oven rooms. How life seems devalued here. Daughters become mothers while yet children—their disease-ridden bodies their only source of income, trapped in cycles of circumstance and choice, shame, abuse and pride.

I cannot help but feel honored, chosen, approved of in the heart of God to be sent to stand in a place so dear to Him. This God-cherished patch of broken earth has become one of my favorite places. Each time I visit, I learn more about encountering heaven while sitting here at the gates of hell.

Maybe this seems a little strange to you. I know it seems strange, at times, to me. I am learning that holy paradoxes are completely normal on this journey. Embracing His mystery is often a doorway into encountering His majesty.

I am no super saint. I simply love being with Jesus, and He really loves being among the least, the last, the lost. The poor in spirit are still blessed with the kingdom of heaven.

The light is fading as I step into the tin shack alleyway and spot a beautiful young woman, heavily made up, sitting in her doorway. While awaiting her next client, she is crocheting a lace table cover, dainty rose patterns joined at the edges. I stand stunned by the irony of such beauty being created amidst such brokenness. Stopping, I look into two scared, lovely eyes set in a delicate face.

"Your work is so beautiful," I tell her in genuine admiration. She smiles and brings me a chair. We begin to share a litany of life and lace.

Less than three feet away from us, the thin tin sheet wall bounces violently as bodies slam into it in a drunken brawl.

Voices scream profanities that are masked only faintly by the mind-numbing disco beat blaring through the windows. But somehow she and I begin to talk as if we are nestled on a quiet porch in the cool of a summer's evening sipping lemonade.

It is a holy moment. We are enfolded in another realm. In the middle of hell, heaven makes an entrance that will not be stopped.

I finger her delicate lace. "You are so pleased with the beautiful things you are creating, aren't you?"

Kaboom, crash, thud. The wall buckles and recovers.

She smiles shyly and gives an almost imperceptible nod of agreement, her hands never missing a stitch.

"Did you know God crocheted you together in your mother's womb like a flawless piece of lace? He created you and thinks you are beautiful. He looks at His workmanship in you and He is pleased. You are so precious to Him. He has so much more for you than you now see."

Her eyes trace the ground even while her fingers continue their nimble artistry. Silent drops leak down her harshly made-up face revealing soft streaks of what lies beneath. I watch the first rays of Jesus' love begin to penetrate her heart even as she stares at the stitches resting on her knees.

"Are you selling your lace?" I ask.

"Oh yes, a set for fifty Sudanese pounds. I only have one complete."

I buy it, of course. It costs me less than twenty U.S. dollars. It is the equivalent of ten men or a full day's work for her.

Perhaps tonight she will be able to shut her door and put a *Closed for Business* sign in the window. Perhaps she will remember His love giving her the dignity of being seen and not condemned. Perhaps the call to embrace her destiny beyond this hellish corner will echo in its holy stillness more loudly than the deafening atmosphere around her. Perhaps when she begins to crochet again, she will remember who she really is.

Meanwhile, I have her lace sitting on my table. It reminds me of who I am. It reminds me why I was created.

After five years of living and serving in the bush of South Sudan, I have fewer answers now than before. The more I learn, the more I realize how much I don't know and how utterly dependent I am on Him. Some might call that the maturation process.

But I do know one thing more now than ever. I am created for encounter. I am created for intimacy with Jesus. I am created to walk with Him in heaven and bring heaven to the earth. I am created to embrace—and encourage—a walk like that of Enoch.

Created for His Pleasure

> By faith Enoch was taken away so that he did not see death, "and was not found, because God had taken him"; for before he was taken he had this testimony, that he pleased God.
>
> But without faith it is impossible to please Him, for he who comes to God must believe that He is, and that He is a rewarder of those who diligently seek Him.
>
> Hebrews 11:5–6

Enoch, that remarkable man of God who walked so closely with Him that he did not die but was simply "taken away," has long been one of my heroes of the faith. I want to be like him when I grow up. The more I come to know about his journey, the more I see reflections of where I hope my own path leads. Could Enoch be an example of living out God's ultimate invitation? Could his life embody a picture of what we are called and invited into today?

I still sometimes forget I am created simply for the pleasure of God. I get overwhelmed with the urgent needs around me. I, too, need to be reminded that I am created for no other reason but to be loved by Him, to know Him intimately and, out of *that* reality, live out my destiny.

Enoch pleased God. I want to understand what that means deep down inside of me. Enoch brought pleasure to the heart of God. Just like Enoch, we, too, are invited to live from the presence of God for the pleasure of God, releasing the promises of God.

I don't know about you, dear reader, but I have a tendency at times to overcomplicate things. Jesus in His kindness is always simplifying things I make too difficult. The reality of heaven is so much closer than often I have seen or realized.

> From that time Jesus began to preach and to say, "Repent, for the kingdom of heaven is at hand."
>
> Matthew 4:17

Jesus tells us to change the way we think since the realm and reality of heaven is so close we can touch it. I heard Ian Clayton, a revelatory Bible teacher and prophetic speaker, once explain it this way. The ancient Hebrews understood that the supernatural world was all around them—the realm that was filled with God's light and the realm that was darkness. Whichever one they turned to by their desire was the reality they would engage.

Desire is a very powerful thing. It sets us on the course of our destiny.

When I live to satisfy the heart desires of Jesus, it releases Him to fulfill mine. When I live focused on His heart, I become what I behold in Him and step into the "more" I was created for. And when I step into oneness in Him, He steps out of me and actually shifts the atmosphere around me to release His kingdom.

In other words, my internal reality determines my external release. Why was Jesus able to speak peace and still the storm? Because He did not have a storm raging on the inside of Him but rather had peace. We will talk more about what to do with storms in the next chapter.

One of the children I used to teach in Sunday school put it like this: "One day Enoch walked so far with Mr. God that it was too far for him to come back. So Mr. God just took him home with Him."

I want to live just as abandoned, just as set apart, just as sold out every day to God as Enoch did. And when it is all said and done, maybe I, too, one day will walk too far with Mr. God to come back.

The Sands of Time

One reason Enoch's story has had such a profound impact on me is that he and I go way back. Do you remember in the second chapter I shared with you some of my experiences in heaven as a seven-year-old little girl?

When I was experiencing heaven with Jesus in that encounter, I met a man with a closely clipped silver beard. He had deep, blue-green twinkling eyes and was wearing a loosely fitting white shirt and pale trousers that made him look as if he were going for a walk on the beach. He stepped forward and looked in my eyes and smiled. His smile warmed me and made my seven-year-old self want to start giggling at the inside joke even when I didn't even know what the joke was.

He then introduced himself to me. He said his name was Enoch. He told me I would learn to walk as he did. At the time I remember thinking, *That sure is a funny name.*

Only years later would I run across him for the first time in the Bible. Wanting to understand his journey has become a theme for me ever since.

In 2010, I was in my room in Uganda taking a day to be quiet and pray. I was not expecting anything specific. I was just happy for some time to spend with Jesus.

As I was journaling, I became intensely aware of God's presence. Because I was learning that when that happens, it is an invitation, I knew I had a choice whether to "lean into it" or keep doing what I was doing. I stopped writing and started to feel the tangible weight of who He was surrounding me.

As I leaned into His nearness, I instantly found myself in what I now understand to be a *trance*.

Allow me to pause this story to explain what I mean by *trance*. I used to hear the word *trance* and the immediate picture that came to mind was of New Age gurus chanting mindlessly. Thus, I assumed that trances were demonic and not for us. You know that I want nothing to do with the demonic.

But then I started looking into the Scriptures. Trances and trance-like states sent from God are found from Genesis to Revelation. I really had to ask the Lord for forgiveness for assuming that, just because I had heard the word used as common vernacular from the occult world, it was wrong in and of itself. God's people used the word long before the New Age movement existed.

Somewhere along the line, however, a "trance" became associated with Eastern mysticism. The Church, rightly wanting nothing to do with demonic practices, wrongly made the same assumption I did: that all trances must be from the devil. And the devil said, "Thanks so much. I'll take those."

Thus he stole from us something that truly belongs to the kingdom of God and relegated it to drug culture, the occult and Eastern religions. He filled it with darkness, and now we tell ourselves it has nothing to do with us. Boo.

The word *trance* in the New Testament is the word *ekstasis,* and it means a displacement of the mind. But this mental displacement does *not* mean setting aside our minds, as in hypnotism. Nor does it mean emptying our minds, as in Eastern meditation practices. Both these practices produce dangerous trance-like states that are demonic in nature. If we empty our mind, or willingly yield them to another source that is not God, demons are very happy to come and fill the void. God never calls us to blank out our minds like that. No, the displacement, or *ekstasis,* is rather an "overwhelming" of our minds *by* God, in which He and what He desires to show us fills our entire focus.

While praying in Joppa in a trance, for example, Peter had the vision that opened the invitation of Jesus and the baptism with the Holy Spirit to Gentiles (see Acts 11:5). We can see here that Peter, though in a trance, was not in a mindless state. Not at all—he was praying. But he was in a state in which his mental awareness was overtaken completely with the presence and purposes of God.

At times when God wants to show us something, as He did Peter, and not have our natural thinking get in the way, He comes in a way that temporarily displaces all mental distractions so that He becomes our sole focus.

So, back to the story. . . . I was suddenly, unexpectedly, so aware of God's presence in my room in Uganda that I was almost disoriented. I knew to stop and wait for whatever He wanted to do.

Instantly, God overwhelmed me, and I was experiencing *ekstasis,* having a vision. I was standing on a long, narrow beach with glistening, crystal-white sand and an ocean lapping at the shore. A vaguely familiar man walked up to me in loose-fitting trousers, white shirt, bare feet, close-trimmed silver beard and the most twinkly blue-green eyes imaginable. In a rush I remembered back to when I was seven.

In the vision, Enoch came and stood beside me facing the ocean. Somehow I knew that, at this shore, the sands of time were meeting the ocean of eternity.

He chuckled and said, looking out to the horizon, "When I first came here, this beach used to be a lot bigger. But the sands of time are being swallowed by eternity. Keep combing the sands of time for the treasures of eternity."

Then he turned and looked me in the eye. "Chin up, girl, you have lots of friends here. We are cheering you on!"

The vision faded rapidly, but the weight of God's presence stayed around me for several hours as the depth of the experience sank into my heart.

Keep combing the sands of time for the treasures of eternity. Enoch lived like that. You and I can, too. It is part of our supernatural destiny.

How do we do this? I have found some ways that I would like to share with you in the rest of this chapter.

A Call for Today

> Enoch, a righteous man, whose eyes were opened by God, saw the vision of the Holy One in heaven, which the angels showed me, and I heard everything from them, and I saw and understood, but it was not for this generation, but for a remote one which is to come.
>
> Enoch 1:2

Enoch lived out of an understanding of God ahead of his day. The vision he carried was for remote generations to come, including our own.

Some of you may wonder why I am quoting extra-biblical literature. The book of Enoch, while not canonical Scripture, was highly recognized and part of the ancient Hebraic worldview. It was so much a part of the contextual fabric of the times that even the New Testament quoted it (see Jude 14).

I believe Enoch is a picture of something God desires to do in our day. The book he wrote gives us a bit more understanding of who he was and how he walked with God. You are reading this book and getting to know a bit more about me and what I have learned. In the same way, I read his book to learn more about him and what he learned.

Jesus once told me, "You can either wander in Egypt or walk like Enoch. Which would you choose?"

I definitely chose the latter. But I wanted insight into what that choice looked like in practical, everyday terms. So I went back to where Enoch was mentioned in Genesis to see what I could find.

Initiation into Intimacy

And Enoch walked with God; and he was not, for God took him.

Genesis 5:24

When I began to study Enoch, I found some amazing things, starting with his very name. We know that names in the Bible are wrapped up with meaning and often paint pictures of God's heart. Nothing in Scripture is there by accident, not even names and genealogies.

Enoch means "initiated," or someone who is initiated into something. This Enoch was one who was initiated into intimacy. *Enoch* also means "to dedicate, to narrow, to train up, to enter in."

When I looked at the meaning of the individual Hebrew letters (pulled from my college notes that I still carry with me for reference on my computer), Enoch's name formed a word picture that could be interpreted as "a gateway of life whose full expression is love, a gateway to unity with God that leads to a multiplication of His kingdom connected to the government carried by a prostrating king (one leading and ruling through humility)."

I want to live my life as a gateway into the life of God, whose full expression is love. I want my life to bring the kingdom of the King who bowed low and became the servant of all. Like Enoch, we, too, are invited into an abiding intimacy with God that is a narrow way.

All over the earth, it seems, things are shaking around us. Famine, war, economies in crisis. It is a critical time to know where we are seated in the heavenly places so that when all earth shakes, we can bring the answers of heaven into the shaking.

Enoch walked in promises ahead of his day. Because he lived a life united with God, who dwells in the place of creative light outside time, Enoch could pull his tomorrow's promise into his present day. As we walk with Jesus, so can we.

I love that Enoch is not remembered for some great miracle or act of power, other than maybe his final disappearing act. He is remembered simply for who he was—one who pleased God. By far heaven's greatest invitation is the one that lands us right in the middle of the pleasure of God.

The Fruit of Humility

Jared lived one hundred and sixty-two years, and begot Enoch.

Genesis 5:18

Enoch was the son of Jared. *Jared* means literally to descend, to go lower still in a picture of humility.

If we would like to walk in such intimacy with God that we are brought into the things of heaven, where our lives usher in His kingdom all around us, our walk itself has to be born out of a choice to embrace humility.

Ongoing, deepening intimacy can only be the fruit of humility—the fruit of desperate dependence on the One who is everything to us.

Launched Out in Love

Enoch had a son whose name was Methuselah. *Methuselah* refers to one who is a missile, a dart, a flaming weapon launched into the darkness.

I see an Enoch company arising in the earth—a company of people whose posture of humility positions them in intimacy that will ultimately produce a movement of fiery burning ones, launched as weapons of light into the darkness. These flaming missiles will carry the glory of God and help set cities and nations ablaze.

They will be gateways of the life of God fully expressed in His love. Bowing low to serve in humility, they will see God's supernatural kingdom break forth all around them.

You and I, dear reader, are invited into all of this. You are not reading these words by accident. Nor am I talking about a generation far off, alive in some remote time period yet to come. No, this is an invitation for you today. It is why I am writing about the lessons I am learning on this journey.

We can wander, trapped in Egypt, in a world system that rebels against God and tries to reach heaven apart from a genuine relationship with Him. Or we can walk like Enoch, choosing the kind of intimacy with God that equips us to walk in earth and heaven at the same time.

Partnering with the Angelic

May I mention one vital portion of understanding that was alive in the early Church but has been largely forgotten by the Church of today? That is an understanding of partnering with the angelic. It is a crucial part of our inheritance that God is restoring in this season.

Enoch, Abraham, Elijah, Ezekiel, Daniel, Mary, Peter and John (just to name a few) all lived in the very present provision of heaven in and through angelic interventions and encounters. Remember, we have been saying that the reality of the kingdom of heaven is as close to us as the air we breathe. We simply need to turn our focus into its supply and presence.

We are often trained (as I mentioned in chapter 4) to turn our attention to the power of darkness more than to the kingdom of God and His light. We read books and books on understanding how the demonic functions. Once again, I am in no way advocating ignorance of the enemy, simply that we keep our focus on the right realm.

I have gone though seasons when I spent my first waking moments each day binding every demon I could think of, in effect, turning my full attention toward what the enemy was doing. It should have been no surprise that such days often unraveled before they began!

Binding every demon I could think of—in essence, greeting the darkness—was considered normal morning protocol in the streams I was in at the time. Sometimes I wonder if we ended up with way more warfare than necessary simply because of where we placed our focus.

After learning a few things the hard way, I decided I wanted God's kingdom to be the first reality I turn my attention to every day. And I do. Now I wake up very intentionally saying good morning to the Father, to Jesus, to the Holy Spirit and to all of the angelic hosts assigned to my life. I turn my focus on His goodness and provision.

Here is what I wonder: If the early Church engaged regularly with the angelic realms—which it did—why do we so often relegate such engagement to story, history or the occult? What happened to bring about such a dramatic change?

I was reminded recently about a piece of Church history that might shed some insight on this question.

Back in the 700s in France, there was what I believe could have started as a genuine move of God's Spirit that brought a renewed emphasis on the supernatural. A Gaullic preacher named Adalbert, who first appeared on the scene in the district of Soissons, was its central character. I am going to venture out on a limb here. Almost all the websites and books I have read about this time period brand this man as a total heretic. And he very well could have been.

I am not defending his theology or practice. In fact, so little is known about him it is hard to tell *what* he actually believed. The recorded history is only told from one perspective, the people who excommunicated and imprisoned him. You and I both know every story has more than one side to it.

What is most interesting to me is *not* who Adalbert or his colleagues were or what they believed. It is how the governmental structure of the church in their day responded to them. Their beliefs may have truly been heretical. It is also possible that they were, at least in part, misunderstood and misrepresented. From the scant history we have, it is really difficult to tell.

But this we do know: The Roman Catholic Church, fearful of heresy and the growing interest in the angelic, shut the whole thing down instead of redirecting specific errors. Could the reaction of the church be equally guilty of doctrinal excess in the opposite direction? I am not a historian, but it is something that makes me wonder.

At the Council of Rome in A.D. 745, Pope Gregory condemned the growing interest in the angelic realms largely because of Adalbert and his followers. As part of the rulings of this council, all previously recognized archangels were called heretical. The only angels permitted to be named within the church after that ruling were Michael, Gabriel and Raphael.

In redirecting ideas that may or may not have been completely in error (again we only have one side of the story), the church made an overarching decree. This decree actually shut down a rich history of angelic reality that believers should, in my view, understand and know how to operate within.

So how do we help restore what was lost? It helps to have a frame of reference with which to start. I do not intend the following to be a comprehensive teaching on the angelic. But a few basic insights might be useful by way of introduction.

- Angels are spiritual beings created by God sent to minister on behalf of those who will inherit salvation (see Hebrews 1:14).

- We can interact with the angelic realm. The Bible contains more than three hundred references to angelic beings, who they are, what they do and how they operate.

- There are many different types of angelic beings and a governmental order to how they function both in heaven and on earth.

- Angels wait for us to step into our places following Jesus. As we worship and follow Him, they are released to function in their assignments around us.

- Angels have names and distinct identities. It is very useful to find out their names and introduce yourself if you run into one. In such an amazing and wonderful circumstance, just say, "Hi, what's your name?" It really is that simple.

- We do not worship angels or pray to them. Nor do we receive doctrine contrary to the Gospel from them. But talking with them when they show up is not worshiping them or praying to them any more than my talking to you over a cup of tea is praying to you.
- We are intended to partner with angels as we walk supernaturally in God's kingdom. We engage what we turn our attention to. We empower what we honor with our focus. It is time to focus, then, not on what we want to avoid but on where we want to go.

Practical Keys: Walking in Two Realms at Once

I am finding some helpful keys as I reflect on who Enoch was. I have taken each one of these points and prayed practically to embrace it in my own walk. Each of us is called into a unique expression of this supernatural life in Jesus. But here are some thoughts that may be helpful in unlocking this expression in and through your own life as you embrace His invitation to walk with Him.

- Humility brings me into greater intimacy, which launches me into destiny. Go lower to go deeper to go farther.
- The entry into the life of God is living in the full expression of His love. Living loved by Him is the entry point into the supernatural life I am created for.
- Being united with God multiplies His kingdom in and through my life. His kingdom does not come by my own efforts and striving.
- Intimacy with God is a choice. It is intentional, not accidental.

- What I focus on, I empower.
- I am created for another realm, one beyond the one I see with my physical eyes. And it is nearer to me than the air I breathe.
- I am called to partner with the angelic and engage the full provision of heaven.
- The government of the kingdom of God is all about His life flowing through love and bringing restoration.

May I pray for you?

Papa, I ask that You would show this dear one the depth of intimacy that is possible with You. I pray that Enoch's life journey would be a shining example of how closely he or she can walk with You. I ask that You would open my friend's eyes to see the reality of the angelic realms, and understand just how near the provision of heaven is, even right now as he or she reads these words. Come, Holy Spirit. Come and ignite a desire for the "greater things than these." Come and direct this dear one's focus into the kingdom of God. Come and help him or her make intimacy with You a very intentional choice every day. Show this child of Yours how to release the government of Your kingdom coming in and through his or her life, restoring the brokenness all around us. Amen.

Discussion Questions and Activation Exercise

- When you hear the name *Enoch*, what images come to mind? What does it mean to you to walk like Enoch?

- Have you ever tried to engage intimacy without first being willing to embrace humility? Did it work? Why not?

- What expressions of love has God showed you recently? How does His love make you feel? Why is living in His love the entry point to experiencing more of the supernatural life?

- Are there areas in which you have tried to bring God's kingdom in your own strength instead of functioning out of a place of intimate connection with Him? What were they? Take those areas back to Him and lay them at His feet. Then lean into His embrace, knowing that every promise comes to pass out of the place of living in His pleasure.

- Do you feel that you are pleasing to God? Why or why not? Bring what you feel before Jesus and ask Him how He feels about you. Do this again for the Holy Spirit and the Father.

- Have you ever experienced the weighty presence of God so thick you felt disconnected from your immediate surroundings? This could have been the beginnings of a trance. If not, ask Him to bring you into that kind of experience. If so, remember it now, and ask God to take you deeper.

- Ask God to reveal the specific angels assigned to you in this season of your life. Write down what He shows you. Practice turning to His kingdom reality every day.

Activation: Have you ever heard about something the enemy has stolen, such as a godly trance or angelic interaction, and then relegated that experience to the "not-for-me" category? Spend some time asking the Holy Spirit to teach you the truth about that experience from the Bible. Because the realm and reality of heaven really is so close we can touch it, allow Him to change the way you think.

8

In Storms and Darkness

It is a day that dawns like any other here in South Sudan. The March 2009 morning quickly goes from warm to hot and has the feel of a brewing storm hanging in the air.

We are still settling in from our recent move onto our new land a few miles from the center of Yei. It is forty acres of freedom for our children after two years of being cooped up on less than a dusty acre of rental property in the middle of town.

For reasons unknown to me, there is a sense of foreboding in my spirit growing like the distant thunderclouds building on the horizon. Soon morning turns to lunchtime, and I notice looks of concern silently being exchanged among our staff. The radio reports a band of the Lord's Resistance Army (LRA), one of the most brutal rebel groups in the world, is less than ten miles away and headed in our direction. Being on the outskirts of town could leave us vulnerable to attack. Worry is etched on our senior leaders' faces.

Around three o'clock, a team member and I go into town briefly to find out the latest information from other agencies and to email a brief prayer request. While we are gone, local governmental officials instruct everyone through a radio broadcast to pull out their machetes and AK-47s and be prepared to fight. Our choices narrow rapidly before our eyes.

Do we stay on our compound with our ninety children and some older mamas protected only by two guards armed with bows and arrows? Or do we evacuate into town and risk spending the night in the open with fearful mobs roaming around with automatic weapons and machetes? Not exactly a win-win situation! I am so happy we live in God's supernatural kingdom.

On the way back to the compound the road is hauntingly reminiscent of a disaster movie scene where everyone else is running the opposite direction. Murmurs of "Run, run, the LRA are coming!" ripple throughout the crowds. Fear hardens their expressions as they stare into the fading evening light. Just as we turn off onto the dirt road leading to our compound, one lone motorbike screeching by, with a woman swinging a machete over her head and shouting, punctuates the dusk horizon. Silently the two of us bounce the rest of the way home, each cocooned in our own thoughts.

A crowd of my children and staff anxiously awaiting the verdict greets me at the gate. Do we stay or go? Our entire neighborhood has fled into town in fear of the terror that stalks in the night. The area has become a virtual ghost town.

I know in my spirit we must stay. I can see the fiery angels of God's presence standing at attention all along our fence.

We will be safe here. I hear Jesus clearly say, "Beloved, I don't want you to run, I want you to worship."

We gather as a family and I announce we will not be running into town like everyone expects. Jesus has said to stay and worship. Questioning looks sweep the crowd. The light is quickly fading around us, and the LRA is known to attack soon after nightfall.

With our staff, we make some minimal arrangements for extra patrols of our older boys to keep watch with our watchmen. Then we all meet in the courtyard to worship together. Soon our nightly love song to Jesus is rising with even greater fervor than normal. The beats of the bamboo sticks on our plastic jerry cans slow, and one by one the children begin dropping to their faces, weeping into the dirt all around me. I lean close to listen to their prayers.

To my astonishment, they are not crying out for our safety: They are crying out for the salvation of the LRA. "Jesus, please let the rebels know You. Let them know they don't have to kill people. Show them Your love and forgiveness."

Grateful tears stream down my face. Into this storm, all heaven invades through the prayers of our children. As they stand back up, we pray together for our eyes to be opened in the Spirit to see what God is doing. There are more with us than could ever be against us (see 2 Kings 6:17).

We wake the next morning and stories from the night come trickling in. We have more reason to celebrate than we know. We find out in bits and pieces that the LRA had been headed straight for us. They had massacred a family and abducted children less than a mile from our compound. For some *unknown* reason, they stopped, turned around and went the opposite direction. Our theory: They saw our angels.

171

The Power of Rest

Six months later, the LRA again returned less than ten miles from us. But this time it was a completely different story. Our staff and children were not even concerned. They had seen what God had done earlier in the year.

When I asked my good friend, our head mama, how she was doing given the situation, her reply was: "We don't live in fear, we live in Jesus. He will care for us. We are not worried this time."

What I didn't know until then was that our children had decided enough was enough. They were tired of the enemy killing people in their backyard. They began to call for early morning prayer meetings in their houses. Getting up at five o'clock, even our little six- and seven-year-olds worshiped and prayed, pouring their hearts out to Jesus.

They asked Jesus to cause the LRA rebels to turn themselves in to the police and then for the police to help these rebels go home and be reunited with their families. My sons and daughters were storming the gates of heaven that the captives in their midst might be set free. I was speechless at the beauty of their hearts.

Truly, it takes no great love to love those who love you. But what great love it takes to love and pray for an enemy that has raped and pillaged and stolen everything from you. They teach me more about His great love every day.

Many of our children were praying not for an impersonal threat, but for the very enemy that had ripped their homes and lives apart. I was watching the miracle of the Gospel in action. I stood as a witness to the love of God that supernaturally transforms from the inside out.

172

Three days later all heaven began to enforce God's response. A group of ten LRA rebels walked into our police station of their own accord and turned themselves in, saying, "We are tired of killing people and stealing; can you help us?"

Dear reader, I probably don't have to tell you this is not a normal occurrence. But in the kingdom of God, even the smallest child's prayers are enough to stop one of the most feared rebel movements on the planet.

Where armies of the earth had failed, the prayers of children that know who they are as sons and daughters of their Father in heaven moved mountains! They did not cry out for vengeance or retribution, but for mercy on their enemies. How heaven must have marveled. I know we did.

The testimony of what God did when He protected us several months prior, as well as what He was doing even as they were praying then, became a legal precedent they could hang their faith on. It became a place of rest from which His will could be established all around them.

Over the next six weeks, spurred on by what they saw God doing, our children continued praying. Forty-seven more LRA rebels turned themselves in to police headquarters in neighboring areas. And just as was prayed, many of the rebels were reunited with their families and repatriated back into their home communities.

My friend, this invitation into the supernatural life isn't just about having experiences. It is about having experiences with God that so profoundly change you and empower you that *you* carry the reality of who He is into the world around you. It is about building a history with Him, where His past faithfulness becomes a legal precedent for your present exercise of faith.

The Place of Government

There remains therefore a rest for the people of God. For he who has entered His rest has himself also ceased from his works as God did from His. Let us therefore be diligent to enter that rest, lest anyone fall according to the same example of disobedience.

Hebrews 4:9–11

When the Bible talks about rest, it is not speaking of taking a nap. Rest is the place from which we can bring the government of God's kingdom to influence and change the situations around us.

Two different words for rest are used in this passage.

The first time rest is used the word is *sabbaton*, which means a "ceasing of work" or a "stopping of activity in mid action." It comes from the Hebrew word *shabbat*, from which we get our word Sabbath.

But every other time the word rest is used in this passage, it is the word *katapauo*. *Katapauo* is a fascinating word. It means *to settle down*, literally *to colonize* or *to create a place for a government to rest*.

Outside of the book of Hebrews it is only used one other time in the New Testament.

"Heaven is My throne, and earth is My footstool. What house will you build for Me? says the LORD, or what is the place of My rest?"

Acts 7:49

The passage in Hebrews 4:9–11 was an enigma to me for a long time. The whole "labor to enter rest" part had me perplexed. I filed it away as one of those odd kingdom paradoxes.

174

It wasn't until after we had that experience with the LRA that I began to realize rest was more than ceasing from something.

We first enter into the Sabbath rest of God, the place where we cease from our own works so that He can establish a place for His government to rest in our lives. Simply put: For us to step into the reality of what Jesus has already done, we must stop trying to do it for ourselves.

The place of rest we labor to enter into is the place where His government is established in every part of our lives, where His kingdom comes and His will is done on earth as it is in heaven in us. Then, when His kingdom rests in us, the supernatural breaks forth through us almost effortlessly.

Sleeping in Storms

And a great windstorm arose, and the waves beat into the boat, so that it was already filling. But He was in the stern, asleep on a pillow. And they awoke Him and said to Him, "Teacher, do You not care that we are perishing?" Then He arose and rebuked the wind, and said to the sea, "Peace, be still!" And the wind ceased and there was a great calm.

Mark 4:37–39

I mentioned in the last chapter how our internal reality governs our external release. Let's talk a little more about how this functions.

Jesus could speak peace to the storm because He did not have a storm raging on the inside of Him. We release the government of what we carry inside of us to operate around us.

Why did He rebuke the disciples for having little faith? I believe it was because they allowed the external storm around them to cause an internal storm inside of them, and then the only thing they had to release into the situation was fear. The most dangerous storms are always the ones that rage within us. In contrast, Jesus demonstrates for us how to operate out of the power of rest even in a raging tempest.

Jesus was curled up sleeping in the middle of the storm because the full reality of the government of God's kingdom was present within Him. When He spoke, He released the peace He carried, which brought a higher government to bear on the storm around Him and changed the situation.

Everything Jesus walked in, dear reader, is absolutely and totally available to us right now, right in the middle of the most turbulent of our present-day circumstances.

God wants to build a place of rest inside us that can contain and release the government of His supernatural kingdom everywhere we go. Then wind, waves and even rebel armies have no choice but to come into alignment to the reality of heaven God desires to unleash in and through our lives.

The Art of Storm Shifting

I once heard Bill Johnson say, "We only have authority over the storms we can sleep through." That started me wondering: If we have authority over storms we can sleep through, what about the storms we can dance in?

A few years ago in the middle of one of our famous rainy season squalls, I was taken into a vision of an army of people arising to dance on a stormy ocean in the middle of the night. Out of the center of their beings beams of light burst forth as they spun and twirled in a symphony of radiance right in the middle of the raging darkness. It was so beautiful even angels stood in awe.

Maybe that is who we are called to be: storm dancers, light carriers.

Storms are inevitable. They come and go. Some come with gentle rain, others with gales of destruction. I am originally from Florida. Every year we have hurricane season there. As a child, I remember nights we were glued to weather reports featuring storm-battered reporters as we waited to see which direction the swirling mass of wind and rain would head.

Windows boarded up, food stored, bathtubs and buckets filled with extra water, batteries and flashlights on hand: We watched and wondered. Being far enough inland to be safe, we were prepared to ride out the impending fury of the season.

I am no stranger to storms. My life has been filled with them. One thing I continue to learn in my own journey is that every storm brings with it an invitation to dance on the waves and let the wind teach you to fly. Every storm carries the opportunity to learn how to stand in its midst and from the place of rest shift its course and outcome.

Storm shifting is a fine art. It is true we only have authority over storms we can sleep in. We only have authority over the storms we view as invitations to radical abandonment and trust. Fear displaces our authority, but living out of rest, being confident in His love sustains and increases it.

How do you shift a storm when the winds rage and waves crash all around you?

My years of watching hurricane seasons come and go taught me something. Large storms have an order to them. Hurricanes blow and churn around an eye, a central undisturbed place of peace in the middle of the chaos. If the eye wall of the storm, the place of order, is disorganized, the storm itself breaks up and disintegrates. Even storms are governed from a place of rest. Wherever this seat of its government moves, the storm's influence moves.

Have you ever been in the eye of a storm? It is surreal. The silence is deafening. Even in the middle of a hurricane, we can find the place of undisturbed rest in Him. And from this place of rest His peace inside of us can bring government to the storm around us, just like the eye of a hurricane.

We stay in the eye of the storm by staying eye to eye with the One who has total power over it. From peace, we then dispel chaos. From the place of light we disrupt darkness. Hidden in love we overcome fear. We walk in stillness and rest as aggressive choices in the face of winds that rage. And then like Jesus we, too, can stop the storm.

Sinking in the Familiar

> And Peter answered Him and said, "Lord, if it is You, command me to come to You on the water." So He said, "Come." And when Peter had come down out of the boat, he walked on the water to go to Jesus. But when he saw that the wind was boisterous, he was afraid; and beginning to sink he cried out, saying, "Lord, save me!" And immediately Jesus stretched out His hand and caught him, and said to him, "O you of little faith, why did you doubt?"
>
> Matthew 14:28–31

Peter was a fisherman. He knew wind and waves. He knew water. His life was spent on and around it. Perhaps the hardest substances to walk in faith on are the ones we know the most about. Perhaps the most difficult storms to have faith in are the ones we are most familiar with.

Peter stepped into a supernatural gravity-defying encounter with Jesus because he answered an invitation. Invitations are such powerful things. Dear reader, where is Jesus inviting you to step out and walk with Him on the seemingly impossible?

Remember, Peter wasn't walking on a glassy sea. That would have been amazing enough. He was walking on storm-tossed waters with high winds and waves buffeting his every move. For an instant, just an instant, his gaze turned from the Person he was trusting to what he knew based on years of experience.

Peter didn't sink because he saw the waves. He couldn't help but see them. He began to sink when he let his past familiarity dictate his present focus and derail his faith with fear.

Peter was not actually walking on water; he was walking on faith. Faith is a substance. It is substantial enough to step out on and change history. Fear is not. Walking on faith causes us to walk beyond the realm of natural limitations. Fear chains us to our past, imprisons us in our present and never lets us step beyond it.

Some of the most challenging places to live supernaturally are right in our own backyards. The most challenging storms to dance in are the ones we know the most about. Storm dancing, water-walking demands our focus be on Jesus, or we risk sinking in familiarity.

But Peter didn't sink. He didn't swim back to the boat in defeat. He turned his gaze from the familiar back to Jesus' face and cried out. Immediately (notice immediately), Jesus picked him up and they walked back together. Peter didn't return in failure. He returned closer and more dependent on the One he walked with by faith.

179

I don't imagine Jesus being at all stern with him when He came to his rescue. The "oh you of little faith" had to have been said with a twinkle in His eye. Peter was walking on the water *with* Him, hello. All the other disciples were still in the boat.

Learning to walk in faith is like learning to walk all over again. I don't chide my eighteen-month-olds for falling down when they are learning to run. I pick them up, spin them around until they forget the fall and tell them how proud I am of them for trying. "Okay, let's go again, honey."

Falling only becomes failing when you refuse to get back up, or let fear keep you in the boat in the future. Falling is only an opportunity to start again afresh. It is never fatal unless we refuse to move beyond it. I daily decide to not let my past interrupt my present or dictate my future.

Peter knew water. What is it that we know that we might be called to abandon of our previous paradigms and learn to walk on in a storm?

What familiar places does Jesus want to teach you to walk supernaturally in?

His calling us to step out of the boat just might become one of the greatest invitations to learn how to walk with Him in this supernatural life.

The Thick Darkness Where God Was

But storms are not the only situations we learn to walk supernaturally in. There is another place we learn how to walk in the faith and intimacy with God that releases His authority to operate around us. It is the place where we encounter Him in darkness.

Then they said to Moses, "You speak with us, and we will hear; but let not God speak with us, lest we die." And Moses said to the people, "Do not fear; for God has come to test you, and that His fear may be before you, so that you may not sin." So the people stood afar off, but Moses drew near the thick darkness where God was.

Exodus 20:19–21

This passage challenges and intrigues me. I believe God desired to meet and speak with all the Hebrew people. But when they saw the lightning, the thunders, the fire, the darkness that surrounded the coming of God, they backed away. "Moses, you go and talk to Him."

I wonder what would have happened if they embraced His coming even when He came in darkness. I know there have been times I, too, have backed away when He came in a way I didn't understand.

There Are Different Kinds of Darkness

Most often we equate darkness with evil. It is true that there is a kingdom of darkness. But the darkness associated with the demonic is only one kind of darkness. It is the absence of light. The darkness surrounding God is a totally different phenomenon.

I want to encounter Him in the thick darkness where He is, in the places I don't understand. I want to embrace His mystery that opens a way for me to encounter His majesty.

More than once in Scripture when God shows up in our realm, darkness is mentioned.

Now when the sun was going down, a deep sleep fell upon Abram; and behold, horror and great darkness fell upon him.

Genesis 15:12

And the pillar of cloud went from before them and stood behind them. So it came between the camp of the Egyptians and the camp of Israel. Thus it was a cloud and darkness to the one, and it gave light by night to the other, so that the one did not come near the other all that night.

Exodus 14:19–20

And He rode upon a cherub, and flew; He flew upon the wings of the wind. He made darkness His secret place; His canopy around Him was dark waters and thick clouds of the skies. From the brightness before Him, His thick clouds passed with hailstones and coals of fire.

Psalm 18:10–12

God met Abram and great darkness fell on him. He came to the Israelites as light but faced the Egyptians as darkness. In the Psalms, God surrounded Himself with darkness and thick clouds went before Him.

All of these passages speak of *theophanies*, or times God comes and visibly manifests Himself in our realm.

What Happens When Realms Collide

We are told in Scripture that God dwells in unapproachable light. So how does the One who dwells in light, who has no darkness in Himself, have darkness around Him, preceding Him? The darkness around Him could not be the absence of light. He is light. So what is it?

I wanted to understand so I asked the Holy Spirit.

182

His reply stunned me, "Beloved, this darkness is not the absence of light, but the interference of light." Wow. I know I didn't make that one up. I did my best to avoid physics class. I still don't do math or numbers. But my curiosity won out over my past aversion to the subject, so I Googled "interference of light."

Google took me to many physics websites with scary-looking formulas on them. I carefully avoided the formulas. But I sure found out something interesting hidden among them.

When you have two waves that meet, one of two things happen. If they are in sync with one another (in other words, their high points and low points match), they amplify each other's strength, and in the case of light, get brighter. If they are out of sync, they in effect cancel each other out, producing the appearance of darkness at the point of their interaction.

Why did this excite me so much? Creation (including light) is out of sync with her Creator. We know this because of what happened when corruption and brokenness entered the world at the Fall.

So when God shows up in the middle of the created world and His perfect creative light interacts with our imperfect created light, it makes total sense why at the point of the interference there is the appearance of darkness. Wow! I love it when science displays more of who God is.

But what if we take this concept even one step further? When we move through the appearance of thick darkness, to step into encountering Him in His realm of light, He changes us so that we are in phase with Him. We become what we behold.

But we all, with unveiled face, beholding as in a mirror the glory of the Lord, are being transformed into the same image from glory to glory, just as by the Spirit of the Lord.

2 Corinthians 3:18

"Let your light so shine before men, that they may see your good works and glorify your Father in heaven."

Matthew 5:16

Then when we step out of the place of intimate interaction with Him, we are now in sync with His light. Which means, His light in us is amplified to shine in the world around us. This, too, is a place of rest, this being in sync with Him.

Could this be one reason all of creation groans and longs for the revealing of the mature sons of God, the ones that have been transformed by and carry His light to transform the world around them? Our invitation into the supernatural life is an invitation to be one with God to such a degree, even creation itself responds to His light and life shining through us.

For the creation was subjected to frustration, not by its own choice, but by the will of the one who subjected it, in hope that the creation itself will be liberated from its bondage to decay and brought into the freedom and glory of the children of God. We know that the whole creation has been groaning as in the pains of childbirth right up to the present time.

Romans 8:20–22, NIV

Practical Keys: Growing in Authority

Dear reader, does the potential of being able to impact the world with the love and power of God excite you as much as it does me? The more we understand how and why God's kingdom works the way it does, the more we can proactively engage it.

How do we grow in authority and experience more of the fullness of God's kingdom? Growing in authority is a process of growing in maturity with Jesus.

Maturing as Sons

For as many as are led by the Spirit of God, these are (mature) sons of God. For you did not receive the spirit of bondage again to fear, but you received the Spirit of adoption (placing as a son) by whom we cry out, "Abba, Father."

Romans 8:14–15, parenthetical notes mine

When we choose to follow Jesus, we are born again into God's family as His children. The Greek word for a child is *teknon*. A *teknon* is an immature child who might be an heir in right, but has not yet been trained to be an heir in experience.

God sends His Spirit into our hearts to help us become mature. The word adoption used here is more accurately translated as *the placing of a mature son*. In the ancient world there was a training process for a child to grow to the point his father could publicly recognize him as a mature son, or a *huios*.

Birth gave the child the right to the father's inheritance, but the time of his placing as a son gave him the ability to participate in that inheritance. It meant the father could trust his son to oversee all that belonged to the family and faithfully represent him in society. The formal recognition of a son's maturity had everything to do with his ability to be trusted with authority.

A child is one born of God, while a mature son is one taught of God. A child has God's nature, but a mature son has His character. This grown-up child looked like his father and intimately understood his father's ways and desires. Growing in authority is the process of being trained by God to carry His likeness as we mature.

When Jesus was baptized heaven opened with the Father's public recognition placing His Son as One who was able to exactly represent Him on the earth.

> And the Holy Spirit descended in bodily form like a dove upon Him, and a voice came from heaven which said, "You are My beloved Son [*huios*]; in You I am well pleased."
>
> Luke 3:22

Even Jesus had to be trained and grow into this expression (see Luke 2:52). So do we. Growing in true authority is a process. It is not a quick fix. It takes time. It takes willingness to surrender and be transformed into Another's likeness. It takes intentional intimacy with Him. We will talk more about growing in intimacy with God in the next chapter.

For as many as are led by the Spirit of God, *these* are mature sons of God. These are the ones who are trusted with His authority and who have full access to participate in His inheritance.

Living by Faith

I have been crucified with Christ; it is no longer I who live, but Christ lives in me; and the life which I now live in the flesh I live by faith in the Son of God, who loved me and gave Himself for me.

Galatians 2:20

Another translation says, "The life which I now live in the flesh, I live *by the faith of the Son of God*" (emphasis mine).

Wow, that one line encourages me so much. Jesus gives me His own faith to live by. This supernatural life, growing in authority and maturity, is not contingent on my having enough faith to make it happen.

Realizing this has been one of the most freeing things in my walk with God.

Dear reader, everything in these pages is for you. Your inheritance in Jesus is a supernatural life lived in the here and now. And God wants to take you on an amazing journey to grow into the full experience and engagement of all that belongs to you as His heir.

May I pray for you?

Papa, would You come right now and show my friend the amazing inheritance that belongs to us in Jesus? I ask that Your call to step out of the boat and walk on water would resound and echo clearly. Let the invitation to encounter who You are in the place where Your realm meets and changes our realm come with power. Show us how to stand in the middle of a storm and shift its outcome. I ask You to take this dearly loved child of Yours into a daily experience of the fullness of everything available in the inheritance of Your household. I ask these things in the full expression of all Jesus is. Amen.

Discussion Questions and Activation Exercise

- If rest is more than ceasing from our works and includes an entering into the government of God's kingdom, how does that change your understanding of what rest looks like?

- Rest and peace are two different things that are often confused. Having rest operating correctly brings the release of peace. How can you see these two dynamics operating in your life? Ask Jesus to show the place of rest He wants to establish inside of you where He wants His government to be formed.

- What familiar areas of your life is Jesus calling you to walk supernaturally in? Take what each one of them shows you and talk with Him about what that means. Allow Him to call you out of the boat to walk with Him on water.

- Has there ever been a time God came around you in a way that you did not understand and you drew back from Him? Take a moment now to recall those experiences and record them.

- Have you allowed God to train and mature you to entrust you with more of His authority? Have you ever said yes to His training process intentionally? If you are willing, take a moment to do so now.

Activation: Every encounter we have with God is an invitation back into encounter. It is an open door that we have a mandated responsibility to actively recall to and engage. We return to previous encounters by faith, allowing the images of the memory to become a place we step into much like we do when experiencing the Scriptures. Then from that place, go deeper, go further and learn more. Maybe no one has told you that your previous encounters with God are supposed to be a primary platform for your present engagement. When I began to realize this truth a few years ago, it opened up so many more ways to meet with God.

Knowing this, pick one of the times when God came and you shied away from the way in which He came. Every time He comes it is an invitation. Ask His forgiveness for not accepting what He extended. Talk with Him about it.

Then using the memory of that experience, step back in by faith to meet with Him and embrace any way He chooses to come.

9

The Councils of the King

Sweet friend, it has been *quite* the last ten days here in South Sudan. Supernatural does not mean super-easy. Nor does it always mean taking ground. Some days it is a matter of holding the ground that has already been taken and refusing to be moved by what your physical eyes see.

As I try to wrap up writing this chapter, our lives here on the compound in Yei are engulfed with dealing with a suspected typhoid outbreak. What better way to introduce staying in the councils of the King than telling you a real-life, real-time, nitty-gritty, down-in-the-dirt account straight from my backyard in Africa? Welcome to my world.

In less than a week, forty of my children have fallen sick with raging fevers and a whole spectrum of nasty tropical symptoms. Ten of them are hospitalized. Thus commences thrice-daily runs to the hospital with more sick children for doctors' visits and bringing meals for those admitted. In Africa as in many parts of the developing world, most hospitals

191

do not provide food or bedsheets. It is usually up to family to provide for loved ones who are sick. Living here gives Jesus' statement in Matthew 25:36, "I was sick and you looked after me" (NIV), a whole different meaning!

Hundreds of dollars not in the budget disappear in fuel costs, exam fees and medical expenses. Looming over us is the threat of impending chaos on the compound as most of us are running on fewer than four hours' sleep a night.

Smack-dab in the center of it all, I am stealing a few seconds on the fringes of my day to share with you this chapter, describing our invitation to bring the government of God's supernatural kingdom to change the world around us. The irony makes me laugh. Or maybe the oddness of my sense of humor is amplified by a week of sleep deprivation.

Yet even in the hardest, most tiring moments, I have known grace. None of this medical chaos has taken God by surprise.

We just *happen* to have the most amazing team of visitors who are fearlessly stepping up to the plate to do whatever needs doing. God graces us with incredible times of worship and a ten-story-high angel (no, that is not a typo) assigned to fight for us, standing right in the middle of our compound. My kids continue to astound us all with their servant hearts. We find a brand-new medical center in town with people who know what they are doing and who are fantastically caring in their approach. And to top it off, an outpouring of love and prayer from around the world overwhelms us with joy.

We missionaries can be pretty smart cookies. We usually know an attack of the enemy when we see it. I don't want to give him my attention, mind you, but his attacks are real. However, we do not fight by ranting and railing at the powers of darkness. We fight by releasing the government of another realm into the circumstances swirling around us.

> "Your kingdom come. Your will be done on earth as it is in heaven."
>
> Matthew 6:10

What does Jesus' kingdom coming look like in the middle of our messy, everyday lives? What about in the middle of a typhoid outbreak in Sudan? That is what this chapter is all about.

Our circumstances often extend their own invitations to embrace crisis. At times like these I must determine resolutely in my heart that I live in Christ, not in crisis. Storms are invitations to dance. I remind myself that my internal reality determines my external release. I want to base my internal reality on the fullness of His kingdom coming in and through my life.

Kingdoms have kings. Kingdoms also have governmental protocols, structures and procedures. God's kingdom is no exception. For us to experience the fullness of what God desires to release through our walk with Him, we need to learn how to function in His kingdom realm.

Friendship with God

All authority in God's kingdom comes through relationship with Him. We are invited first and foremost to be His friends. As I said in the last chapter, in order to grow in authority, we must grow in maturity and intimacy with Him.

God wants to make all He is doing known to us. He longs for close, intimate friendship with you and me. Jesus told His disciples that everything He heard, received and understood from His Father, He made known experientially to them.

> "No longer do I call you servants, for a servant does not know what his master is doing; but I have called you friends, for all things that I heard from My Father I have made known to you."
>
> John 15:15

Jesus gave His life not for a boardroom strategy or a business plan but so that we can become His bride and live as His friends. His invitations still astound me. We cannot accurately understand or apply supernatural experiences outside of an ongoing intimate relationship with God. This is the foundation for fruitfulness in His kingdom.

> So the LORD spoke to Moses face to face, as a man speaks to his friend. And he would return to the camp, but his servant Joshua the son of Nun, a young man, did not depart from the tabernacle.
>
> Exodus 33:11

> And the Scripture was fulfilled which says, "Abraham believed God, and it was accounted to him for righteousness." And he was called the friend of God.
>
> James 2:23

Do you want to be like Moses, who spoke face-to-face with the Lord? I do. Even more, I want to be like Joshua, who refused to leave the Tabernacle. And, like Abraham, I want to be called the friend of God. God tells His secrets to His friends.

The secret of the LORD is with those who fear Him, and He will show them His covenant.

Psalm 25:14

The Amplified Bible puts it this way:

The secret [of the sweet, satisfying companionship] of the Lord have they who fear (revere and worship) Him, and He will show them His covenant and reveal to them its [deep, inner] meaning.

From my own studies using various lexical aids, this passage could literally read that the counsel and intimacy of the Lord are for those who stand in reverent awe of Him. And because of this experience in union with Him, being bound together with Him, He will make them intimately know the place of His covenant.

Our entire supernatural journey with God hinges on cultivating intimacy with Him. Without that, we have no foundation on which to build anything else. True kingdom authority is rooted in one place: an ongoing, deepening friendship with the Person of God Himself.

Treasuries of Wisdom and Knowledge

"The fear of the LORD is the beginning of wisdom, and the knowledge of the Holy One is understanding."

Proverbs 9:10

There are three words in this passage that we use almost interchangeably in modern usage, but which have very distinct meanings in their original context: *wisdom, knowledge, understanding.* Sometimes we really do lose important things in translation. Living overseas for most of my adult life has taught me that lesson well. So let's take care with three vital words.

Wisdom is skill, practical application and discernment. *Knowledge* is not intellectual, theoretical information but intimate, experiential knowledge. *Understanding* means both the ability to put concepts together mentally and distinguishing between these concepts, separating them out.

Where do all skills, practical application and discernment begin? With the reverential awe of the Lord. Intimate experiential knowledge of the Holy One is the ability to rightly separate and put together the things we learn. True wisdom cannot exist outside of relationship with God.

Trying to gain understanding apart from intimacy with Him is choosing to follow in the steps of Adam and Eve at the Fall. A big no.

There is so much God wants to share with us as His friends. Learning from Him should be our first choice, not our last resort.

> . . . that their hearts may be encouraged, being knit together in love, and attaining to all riches of the full assurance of understanding, to the knowledge of the mystery of God, both of the Father and of Christ, in whom are hidden all the treasures of wisdom and knowledge.
>
> Colossians 2:2–3

The word used for *treasures* here can also be translated as treasuries, storehouses or repositories. In Him are literal treasuries, storehouses of wisdom and knowledge. We can experience them, as you know, only through our relationship with Jesus.

It is through this relationship that we are invited into the counsels of God, where we receive what we need to bring His answers to the situations around us. I don't know about you, my friend, but I am always in need of more guidance and wisdom to bring heaven's reality into the circumstances of my world, with or without typhoid epidemics. You, too?

Let's take a closer look at how we access and engage the treasuries stored inside of His heart.

In the Cellar of Wine

It was the final session of a conference I was speaking at in the south of England. God's presence had come powerfully all weekend long. I was one of two speakers and we alternated meetings. This last service on the final evening of the event was the other speaker's turn to minister.

While he spoke, the heavenly realm entered the room. I don't quite know how to describe it except perhaps as a tangible atmosphere. The speaker had been preaching very coherently and then something shifted.

Try as he might, he could not get words out that made sense unless he ministered prophetically—saying what he heard God say in the moment, speaking spontaneously and directly into people's lives, both individually and corporately. God had hijacked his sermon.

The cloud of God's presence that came into the room made the air feel very thick, almost as if we could slice it. His weighty love rested around us like a blanket. It reminded me of Paul's admonition in Ephesians 5:18: "Do not be drunk with wine, in which is dissipation; but be filled with the Spirit." There are times when the Holy Spirit so moves in and around us that His coming seems intoxicating.

This kind of experience is what some streams refer to as being "drunk" in the Spirit. But maybe you prefer to think about a strong sense of God's presence in another way. Since I am not sure where your own journey has taken you, I do not want terminology to be a stumbling block for you. There is a lot of vernacular out there to choose from, and God is bigger than all of it!

But truly, there is a place of meeting Him where words are superfluous, where it is enough just to be in Him, to be with Him, to be His. Of all the ways I encounter Him, soaking in His weighty presence is one of my favorites. Remember, too, what Jesus said:

> "Whoever drinks the water I give them will never thirst. Indeed, the water I give them will become in them a spring of water welling up to eternal life."
>
> John 4:14, NIV

In that final session of the conference, when God was making His presence felt so strongly, I found myself drinking the living water Jesus gives until it bubbled up like a spring inside of me, giving me enough to give away to a thirsty world.

At the very end of the service, we had a time when the speaker was praying for people. I absolutely did not expect him to come pray for me. I had my eyes closed and was simply enjoying sensing how God was moving in the room. Next thing I knew, the speaker was standing before me.

He said just two words. It was a Holy Spirit sneak attack. Two words, when God is breathing on them, are all it takes.

The speaker's voice boomed over me: "Governmental authority."

Before I knew what hit me, I was unceremoniously flat on my face. It was like when I was a little girl playing in the ocean, an unexpected wave hit, and I found myself tumbling in a force much stronger and bigger than myself.

This time Jesus' presence came so sweetly, so intensely, that I lost all sense of anything but Him. I could barely get two thoughts of my own to connect to even ask, "What's going on here?" My inquiry was probably more like, "Huh, God?"

He replied to my barely formed question, "Beloved, governmental authority is found in the wine realm of heaven."

My response again was a very profound, "Uh, huh?"

The meeting ended a few hours later, the people went home and I was still unable to get up because of the weight of God's presence on me. My friends had to carry me out to the car and into their house. This experience continued for two days.

When the intensity of it began to ebb, I started to ask the Holy Spirit questions about the connection between governmental authority and this "wine realm of heaven." I always want to find out the scriptural context for my encounters with God.

From Colossians 2:2–3 again,

> . . . that their hearts may be encouraged, being knit together in love, and attaining to all riches of the full assurance of understanding, to the knowledge of the mystery of God, both of the Father and of Christ, in whom are hidden all the treasures of wisdom and knowledge.

I needed "the full assurance of understanding." The Greek word for *understanding* in this passage means a mental putting

together. Understanding birthed out of a place of holy intimacy would allow me to retain the substance of what I had
experienced. The Lord helped me to put together several key
ideas about what He had spoken into my life.

First He reminded me of Revelation 17–18 about Babylon,
"with whom the kings of the earth committed fornication,
and the inhabitants of the earth were made drunk with the
wine of her fornication" (Revelation 17:2). I could clearly see
Babylon portrayed as an entity that intoxicates the nations
with the wine of her immorality.

Babylon is a type of a false governmental world system, a
demonic spiritual government. Intoxication with false wine
brings a false governmental authority rooted in adultery and
idolatry, which is false intimacy.

But in Scripture, I knew, if there is a false wine, there must
also be a true. The next place the Holy Spirit had me read
was Song of Solomon 2:4:

> He brought me into the cellar of wine.
>
> DOUAY

> He hath brought me to the house of wine, and his banner
> over me is love.
>
> DARBY

My heart leapt. This is what Jesus was talking about! Here
I saw a picture of being invited into the cellar of wine. Some
translations say "banqueting table," but the literal translation is "house of wine." This is the place of deep and joyful
intimacy where He unfurls love, His banner, over us.

In the ancient world, I learned, banners were visible displays, emblems and announcements of governmental identity

200

and authority, especially on the battlefield. In the house of His wine, God unleashes the governmental authority of His kingdom over our lives. And this authority is rooted and grounded in His love.

What amazing grace is this? Wow, God. The King reveals His heart to His friends! I am getting it, Holy Spirit. Let me be one of those friends.

What am I learning? That I need less thinking in my own limited perspective and more drinking in His. I don't know the full significance of the word I received. But true authority, I have discovered, is found and revealed in the place of intimacy with Him.

In the House of Wisdom

A few months later, I was preparing to visit friends in New York City and share informally with some contacts at the United Nations about the situation in Southern Sudan. As you can imagine, I was praying for greater insight from the counsels of the Lord.

During this time a friend brought Proverbs 9 to my attention.

> Wisdom has built her house, she has hewn out her seven pillars; she has slaughtered her meat, she has mixed her wine, she has also furnished her table. . . . As for him who lacks understanding, she says to him, "Come, eat of my bread and drink of the wine I have mixed."
>
> Proverbs 9:1–2, 4–5

Wisdom has a house! When we read passages like this, they are not just nice poetic literary metaphors; they are invitations into the realities of which they speak. It was very interesting to me to say the least that here wisdom invites us to drink her wine when we need understanding.

My attention was also drawn to the pillars of her house mentioned in this passage. The word pillar there can also be translated platform. I asked the Holy Spirit what the seven pillars or platforms of wisdom's house were. Immediately He reminded me of the verse in James 3 about heavenly wisdom.

> But the wisdom that is from above is first pure, then peaceable, gentle, willing to yield, full of mercy and good fruits, without partiality and without hypocrisy.
>
> James 3:17

These are the hallmarks of wisdom from heaven that come out of the place of intimacy with God and stand in direct contrast to the wisdom that is earthly, sensual and demonic. Again the fruits of our lives will show the source of the wisdom we turn our focus in toward.

God desires us to walk in His understanding that is utterly supernatural. He has answers for the deepest, darkest, hardest situations of our day. We simply need to ask Him to take us into the places where these treasures are stored.

In His Council

Any revelation or understanding God releases through us with power, He first works in us. There is a process that enables us to carry the call and become the message we are called to bring. True understanding *only* comes through intimacy with Him.

Why do I keep reiterating this point? It is just that important.

> My heart within me is broken because of the prophets; all
> my bones shake. I am like a drunken man, and like a man
> whom wine has overcome, because of the LORD, and because
> of His holy words.
>
> Jeremiah 23:9

Jeremiah talks about the overwhelming nature of God's words that produced in him a state like drunkenness. Yeah, Jeremiah, I relate just a little bit!

Jeremiah's heart was broken because of the state of the prophets around him, who were speaking visions of their own hearts to the people. They were not standing in the council of the Lord or hearing His word. They were speaking forth their own words and attaching God's name to them. They were speaking false dreams, lies that perverted and twisted God's truth, and they were stealing words from one another.

Their utterances were not birthed in the place of intimacy with God but in the place of performance and competition. It was one big mess. This is at a minimum sobering stuff to consider even today.

> "I did not send these prophets, but they ran. I did not speak
> to them, but they prophesied. But if they had stood in My
> council, then they would have announced My words to My
> people, and would have turned them back from their evil way
> and from the evil of their deeds."
>
> Jeremiah 23:21–22, NASB

My friend, we are called to bring the truth of who God is to minister life to the world we live in. But we absolutely have to stay in the place of His councils where we receive His words, His understanding and His revelation. We cannot run with our own.

If God does not speak, we remain silent. If He does not send us, we remain still. But if we remain in His council, we have the opportunity to announce His words and bring forth His kingdom transformation around us.

Governmental Decrees

Any functioning government in the natural arena has legal structures and procedures. There are places where laws and decrees are legislated and made. There are places where these decrees are enacted and enforced to bring change in situations that are not aligned to them. God's kingdom is no different.

A crucial part of being effective in bringing His kingdom supernaturally is the understanding of how to operate within its structures and protocols.

Remember in chapter 4 where we talked about the myth of not judging? The reason this myth exists is largely because there is a widespread lack of understanding of the way God's government works. I promised there we would talk in greater detail about this in chapter 9. And here we are!

I am not speaking some esoteric theory. I am speaking of absolute real-world practicality. These truths are how we have dealt with the spiritual dimensions of the typhoid-like outbreak on our compound this week. I will tell you more specifically what that adventure looked like in just a little bit.

So many times we rail against the enemy, coming at him on his own level. We pick a fight on his own turf in darkness instead of spending time in heaven and then bringing light down on top of his head. Then we wonder why the demonic realm beats us up, and we lament about spiritual backlash. Many times backlash is the result of us not knowing what we are doing in the realm of the Spirit.

We need to know the full scope of all we have access to in Christ. It is so much more effective to enter into what Jesus has already purchased for us on the cross, engage the places of God's governmental decrees in heaven and then bring the reality of God's kingdom down with us.

Legislative Protocols

The spiritual world operates on laws just as the physical world does. God's legal decrees win. He has a higher government. The enemy has no choice but to bow out in defeat when God's government is enforced.

> "I will give you the keys of the kingdom of heaven; and whatever you bind (declare to be improper and unlawful) on earth must be what is already bound in heaven; and whatever you loose (declare lawful) on earth must be what is already loosed in heaven."
>
> Matthew 16:19, AMP

Jesus gives us some insight in Matthew 16:19 as to how this legislative structure works. What is bound or loosed on earth, in the seen world, must first be what is bound or loosed in heaven. It is vital to understand what was bound and loosed at the cross for us and what is lawful in heaven. The cross was a place of legal transaction and exchange where we are totally set free and restored.

> . . . having wiped out the handwriting of requirements that was against us, which was contrary to us. And He has taken it out of the way, having nailed it to the cross. Having disarmed principalities and powers, He made a public spectacle of them, triumphing over them in it.
>
> Colossians 2:14–15

We enforce legal decrees on the earth through the power of our agreement. Our words create, define and frame the boundaries for our worlds.

When we agree with darkness, even unintentionally through a turning in toward fear, we empower it to operate. But when we agree with what God says in heaven and line our words up accordingly, we empower His government to operate in our midst.

Many times our team in Sudan does outreach in some very challenging places. We drive hours over nonexistent roads into unstable areas. One day, our base manager and I were driving back from a city about six hours to our north. We were talking and somehow took a wrong road.

Engrossed in conversation, we didn't fully realize the situation until about two hours into the drive when it became obvious we were on the wrong side of a familiar mountain range, and we were passing no known landmarks. We then had a choice. We could panic because we were on an unknown road going in what appeared to be the wrong direction. It looked like we were heading straight into the Congo, in fact. Or we could pray and see what God was saying.

Both of us had a clear sense to keep driving. So we did. With full assurance of faith, I thanked Papa for translating us right to where we needed to be when we needed to be there. After a total of six hours driving on an unfamiliar road going in an unknown direction, never passing one familiar anything, we mysteriously rounded a bend and just "popped out" right at our city gate.

Papa very graciously (and miraculously) got us where we needed to be when we needed to be there as we trusted Him and agreed with the full provision available to us in His kingdom realm.

Judicial Protocols

There are several scenes in the Bible that picture the judicial dynamics that go on in the spiritual world. One of the clearest is found in Zechariah.

> Then he showed me Joshua the high priest standing before the Angel of the LORD, and Satan standing at his right hand to oppose him. And the LORD said to Satan, "The LORD rebuke you, Satan! The LORD who has chosen Jerusalem rebuke you! Is this not a brand plucked from the fire?" Now Joshua was clothed with filthy garments, and was standing before the Angel. Then He answered and spoke to those who stood before Him, saying, "Take away the filthy garments from him." And to him He said, "See, I have removed your iniquity from you, and I will clothe you with rich robes."
>
> Zechariah 3:1–4

Here Joshua (the high priest, not the protégé of Moses) was being accused and attacked by Satan in a scene right out of a heavenly legal drama. The Lord turns to the devil

207

and rebukes him. Right in front of the one bringing the accusation, the judgment of God totally restores Joshua and removes his iniquity. Instantly there is no room left for any accusation to rest. Case closed.

When the enemy tries to accuse us, often we try to ignore the accusation or battle against it in our own strength. Whatever we are battling usually becomes the centrality of our focus. Instead, when accusation or attack comes, we have the option to deal with it judicially according to the reality purchased for us by Jesus on the cross. Then we make Him the One we fix our gazes on and empower.

> "Agree with your adversary quickly, while you are on the way with him, lest your adversary deliver you to the judge, the judge hand you over to the officer, and you be thrown into prison."
>
> Matthew 5:25

In this verse, Jesus seems to be talking about a human adversary. Or is He? These few lines are sandwiched between admonitions on forgiveness and not falling into sin. The word used for adversary in this passage, while it could speak of a human opponent, is also used for Satan (see 1 Peter 5:8).

Jesus tells us we should agree with our *adversary* even while we are on the way with him so we don't wind up in prison. Like many things in Scripture, there are multiple layers of application that are relevant. For our purpose here, I want to explain how it ties in with the passage of Zechariah 3 above.

Matthew 5:25 is not talking about legislative protocols, which deal with releasing the decrees of God with our words, but judicial protocols where we allow God Himself to restore and defend us. When we stand under the government of the

208

Word of God released at the cross, judgment for us is always about restoration and the cutting off of the accusation or attack of the enemy.

Practically, what does this all look like? Well, my friend, have you ever had a time when the enemy came to accuse and condemn you in your thoughts? You know those pesky little thoughts that come: *You're no good. You'll always be alone. They don't really love you; they don't even know you. You are such a hypocrite.* And so on.

If we start immediately rebuking those thoughts, before we know it we are totally focused on every little thing this demon is whispering. Yes, more often than not, those thoughts are a demon speaking lies. Again, what we focus on, we empower.

When Jesus tells us to agree with our adversary, He is not necessarily meaning to agree with the content of the accusation. It means to be at peace with the accuser. In other words, don't fight back. Don't get into a shouting match with the devil. Or you might just wind up in more bondage.

Instead, we can immediately by faith engage the judicial protocols of God's kingdom and come and stand before the Lord in all our brokenness under the covering of the entirety of what Jesus purchased for us at the cross. We don't make ourselves clean. He does.

All we have to do is come into His presence and bring our adversary and the accusations with us. *Oh, really, demon. Hmm. . . . Okay, let's go stand before the Lord with that.*

In Jesus, we are judged as righteous, any soiled garments exchanged and the Lord rebukes the accuser for us. In so doing, He separates us completely from the accusation's effects and enforces the reality of His government in our lives.

Practical Keys: Functioning in Kingdom Protocols

While all of this is amazing insight, how do we actually apply these protocols when we have to deal with the enemy on a larger scale? Let's take this recent outbreak of what looked like typhoid fever on our compound as a case study of sorts.

Typhoid is a disease caused by bacteria. It is spread because of poor sanitation and contaminated water supplies. It is also very hard to test for out here in the bush. But whatever sickness our family was dealing with had similar symptoms and appeared to be carried through our water supply.

Before I address how we dealt with the spiritual side of what was happening, I want to assure you we implemented commonsense strategies in the natural as well. We chlorinated our drinking water, enforced hand washing stations, reminded our children about good hygiene and got the appropriate medical care to those who fell ill.

A multifaceted problem calls for a multifaceted solution.

1. Recognize the Operation of the Enemy

As our children began to get sick in record numbers, our missionary team and I could see this was more than the normal rainy season cycle of illness. I was sitting on a mat with our younger children, holding my babies, asking Jesus what was going on. I do not automatically assume when things go wrong it is an all-out demonic attack. But when a cluster of things goes significantly wrong, I begin to ask questions.

As I sat in the fading evening light, holding eighteen-month-old baby Blessing, I asked Jesus to show me the source of this outbreak. Immediately, in the Spirit, I began to hear low

210

methodical drum beats. Just as heaven carries an atmosphere, so do the forces of darkness. I could feel the demonic stirring.

"What is that I am hearing, Jesus?"

"Beloved, a demonic tribunal of war has been called against the ministry here."

And just like heaven has governmental structure, so does hell. In other words, there was a serious attack being launched against us in the spirit. I knew then it would not be enough to deal with the natural causes of the sicknesses on the compound; we also had to deal with the demonic assignments that were empowering them.

In my past, I would have immediately started a sparring match with the demonic world coming against the lives of our children. I mean, seriously, you do *not* touch our kids. Fortunately, I am learning much more effective ways to deal with the onslaught of the enemy, ways that are rooted in understanding the governmental protocols of the kingdom of heaven.

> So shall they fear the name of the LORD from the west, and His glory from the rising of the sun; when the enemy comes in like a flood, the Spirit of the LORD will lift up a standard against him.
>
> Isaiah 59:19

When the enemy comes to steal, kill and destroy, like an overwhelming flood, the Spirit of the Lord will lift up a battle standard, a banner of His governmental authority against him.

2. Turn Your Focus to God in Worship

That night I gathered the children together, and we had a powerful time of worship. In the middle of worship, at

211

precisely the same moment, one of our missionary team members and I saw the exact same thing happen in the spiritual world around us. A huge bolt of lightning came down from heaven and light exploded in all directions on our compound as our children poured out their hearts to Jesus. The lightning left behind it an enormous angel who stood in the center of our compound, assigned to fight on our behalf.

As you can imagine, this was hugely encouraging for all of us, especially when the medical situation deteriorated within hours and the battle intensified. The next night I called a few of our core leaders together in my house for a time of prayer, the same small block house where my teakettle whistled wild on the night our independence was announced. I explained very simply about the legislative and judicial protocols we have been talking about. As a group, we began to posture ourselves in the presence of God.

We very deliberately fixed our gaze on who He is, not on the problems screaming for our attention. Singing love songs to Jesus, praying in all the myriad of languages we had to pray in between us, thanking Him for His goodness and faithfulness, we waited and worshiped until He completely filled our focus.

3. Engage the Judicial Realm of Heaven

By faith we stood before the Lord and took the attack of the enemy coming against us before Him. Standing under the provision of what Jesus had done for us at the cross, we asked the Father to judge any broken thing in us or our land that was not lining up to His kingdom. Remember in Jesus, judgment is for restoration and the removal of anything that would allow a curse or attack of the enemy to remain.

Father, here we are before You, in faith standing under the full provision of Jesus and what He did on the cross. We ask that any broken thing in us or in our land that gives room for this attack of the enemy be judged right now.

As we waited before Him, together each of us began to hear several different areas that may have given the enemy access. As each area came up we dealt with it.

Father, we take responsibility for allowing this area to operate. We are sorry and ask Your forgiveness. Please judge its brokenness in us that has allowed the enemy to have a point of entry. We thank You for Your forgiveness and restoration through Jesus. Make us whole and close in any gaps or openings to the enemy.

When each area was dealt with and through what Jesus has done, we were *judged* righteous and whole; then we began to deal with the enemy.

Father, we ask You with the same judgment You have judged us with that You judge this attack of the enemy coming against us.

Outside of Jesus, God's judgment brings destruction and cuts the work of the accuser off.

The reality of the matter is everything we need has already been done by Jesus on the cross and is freely available to us. This is simply one practical way of intentionally appropriating it.

We took the reality of the judicial decrees of the Father about our situation and, in faith, said to the demonic world coming against us, "Read 'em and weep, guys. A higher government has trumped yours. You are out of here." They had no choice but to bow.

4. Receive the Full Exchange of What Was Purchased at the Cross and Legislate Restoration

Together our little group thanked Jesus for all He had done and received the full exchange of restoration from Him for every work of destruction the enemy tried to bring in the lives of our family. We then in faith began to release His legislative decrees of restoration by speaking life and healing into our situation.

Father, we thank You that your promise says that by the stripes of Jesus we are healed (see Isaiah 53:5). *We thank You that You have promised us no evil shall befall us, nor shall any plague come near your dwelling* (see Psalm 91:10). *We thank You that You are sending forth Your word right now to heal all who are sick on this compound* (see Psalm 107:20).

I guess we were a little loud because before we were done there was a crowd of my children peering curiously in my windows. I invited them in—there were about fifteen of them—and we all took Communion together as a family, thanking Jesus for the full provision of healing in His blood shed for us. The joy of the Lord and the inebriation of His presence filled the room so powerfully that my kids asked if we could please do it again. Of course we can.

The next morning there were significantly fewer new cases of typhoid, and the situation began to turn around. Now we still needed to do things in the physical world to treat those who were ill, care for those who had been admitted to the hospital and prevent the further spread of the disease. But when we stepped into the legal reality of what Jesus had done on the cross by faith, together with an amazing outpouring of prayer from all over the world, the demonic powers feeding into the situation were utterly defeated.

This is what I mean when I said we don't fight by railing at the demonic world. We fight by releasing the government of another realm into the circumstances around us.

And in Jesus, no matter what comes against us, we win. Game over. Jesus: All. Typhoid: Nothing.

May I pray for you?

Papa, I ask You right now to begin to take this dear one into a place of experiencing what it means to be Your friend. Take this one reading into a deepening place of intimacy with You from which understanding of Your kingdom and how to walk in the fullness of its provision in every area of life may flow. Together we pray, Your kingdom come, Your will be done on earth as it is in heaven all around us. Amen.

Discussion Questions and Activation Exercise

- What does it mean to be God's friend? What does His friendship look like to you?

- What is your current concept of authority? Where does it come from? How does this idea line up with the concepts of maturity and intimacy we have shared about?

- Wisdom, knowledge and understanding are words we do not distinguish sufficiently in the same way the languages of the Bible did. Ask the Holy Spirit to teach you about the nuances between them and what their importance is. Ask Him to show you the treasuries where they are stored in Christ.

- Has there ever been a time God came in a way that made you feel intoxicated by His love or inebriated in

His presence? If so, step back into that memory and ask Him to help you sense His presence even more strongly. If not, ask Him to come to you in that way now.

- How do you tend to fight when the enemy comes against you? How might the understandings shared in this chapter help you be more effective?

Activation: Pick a situation in which the enemy has come against you recently to accuse you in your thought life. Apply the protocols discussed in this chapter to deal with his accusations governmentally instead of defensively.

10

Holy Lightning Rods
and Burning Signposts

It is September 2006. I am staying in a little third-floor room in a dilapidated building in inner-city Johannesburg, South Africa. I was just sent out from Iris Ministries' main base in Pemba, Mozambique, to start a new work in Sudan. As I was leaving, Papa told me to stop and pray in South Africa for three weeks before journeying onward.

It is still winter and the building I have wound up staying in has no heat. I never thought it was possible to be cold in Africa, but I have prayed with my teeth chattering for days now. Again it has been a process of pressing in with faith and obedience. Nothing much visible has happened or changed around me yet. But I understand now more about the quiet seasons, so I am not all that concerned.

It is the evening of the 21st day of my stay here. I sit on the bed shivering under blankets, taking a break from willing my icy fingers to type email responses. Working hard to ignore the mice scuttling around the periphery of the room's threadbare carpet, I decide to read a booklet I have just downloaded from the Internet called *Adventures in God*. It is the first person account of John G. Lake's time in Africa.

John G. Lake has long been one of my heroes. I have marveled at the stories of a man who so knew the healing power of God, he told terrified doctors to put live plague germs on his hand. And while the doctors watched under a microscope, the life of God he carried eradicated the germs right in front of their eyes. Yes, please, Papa. I want to carry Your life like that.

He was part of a revival in South Africa during the last century that saw well over 100,000 people come to Jesus in five years' time. His life is known for amazing healings and creative miracles as well.

I find out several days ago the place I am staying in, as rustic as it is, is less than two miles from where the epicenter of this revival was. I could literally walk to his house if I wanted to. This is really beginning to feel more and more like a divine setup.

I cradle a hot cup of tea in my hands and read:

You talk about the voltage from Heaven and the power of God! Why there is lightning in the soul of Jesus! The lightnings of Jesus heal men by their flash!

John G. Lake

All at once my silent three weeks of "not much" happening is transfigured.

The presence of Jesus begins to build around me, preceding His stepping out of eternity into this worn little upper room right off of Commissioner Street. There are times His comings are quiet, gentle encounters on the fringes of our awareness. This was *not* one of them.

I see the glorified Jesus of Revelation 1:14–15, with eyes of fire and hair white as new-fallen snow, step into my room. Out of the center of His being come blue-white flashes of lightning that shoot through the room and fill it with the electricity of heaven. I literally dive off the bed and lie facedown, shaking on the floor. I understand now *why* John fell as dead at His feet (see Revelation 1:17).

Jesus starts to explain to me, "Beloved, I carry the lightning of heaven in My very being. Why? Lightning is a place where heaven finds agreement with the earth. The life I lived on earth was lived in perfect agreement with heaven. As when I walked the earth, so now with My Body, so now with you. You are called to carry the lightning of heaven as I live in you and you live in Me."

Wave upon wave of His liquid light pulses through me as time is overshadowed by eternity. For four hours, I am with Him. It feels like seconds.

I see vessels being filled with His glory all over the earth— lights arising and shining with His unstoppable love. I see these light carriers journeying on a moving highway into the heart of God. Each beat of His heart draws more of them into His heart and then thrusts them forth to carry His heartbeat to the nations.

When the intensity of His presence lifts, and I become aware again of the mice scurrying along the room's far wall, I know I have just had a destiny-defining encounter with the King. His lightning had flashed through me, and I would not be the same.

Carrying the Lightning of Heaven

This encounter was more than a pivotal moment for my own personal journey. I believe it is filled with heaven's invitation for all of us to walk in the full demonstration of the supernatural power Jesus walked in on the earth.

Let's talk a little more about lightning.

What we see as cloud-to-ground lightning is formed through an invisible electrical charge that first reaches up from the earth and forms a point of contact for the sky. So when lightning's majestic blue-white light rips open the atmosphere on its journey earthward, we are actually watching heaven's visible response to earth's invisible reach. Lightning is a place where heaven has found agreement with the earth and thus can release its power.

God is looking for places of agreement on the earth to unleash His kingdom in and through. This challenges me. Will I allow Him to do what is needed in me so that my life agrees with heaven and becomes a contact point for His release?

A few weeks after that encounter with the lightning of God in South Africa, I found myself in Tororo, Uganda. Upon my arrival there I was told Tororo has the dubious distinction of being *the* lightning strike capital of the planet. It has per year more lightning strikes than any other place on the planet. Somehow, knowing Jesus, I didn't think my being there was a coincidence.

I had gone to share with a regional gathering of pastors. Can you guess what my topic became? I bet you can. In preparing to share about carrying the lightning of heaven at this meeting, I started to dig in to find out more about what Scripture had to say about the matter.

And while He was praying, the appearance of His face became different, and His clothing became white and gleaming.

Luke 9:29, NASB

This passage is the account of what happened at the Transfiguration when Jesus went up into the mountain and met with Moses and Elijah. The word *gleaming* means "to flash like lightning." Wow.

That is just one reference concerning the lightning of God. Here are a few more:

Then it came to pass on the third day, in the morning, that there were thunderings and lightnings, and a thick cloud on the mountain; and the sound of the trumpet was very loud, so that all the people who were in the camp trembled.

Exodus 19:16

Out of the brightness of his presence bolts of lightning blazed forth.

2 Samuel 22:13, NIV

The voice of the LORD strikes with flashes of lightning.

Psalm 29:7, NIV

His lightnings light the world; the earth sees and trembles.

Psalm 97:4

And from the throne proceeded lightnings, thunderings, and voices. Seven lamps of fire were burning before the throne, which are the seven Spirits of God.

Revelation 4:5

Are these references just poetic imagery for the power of God, or are they also an intense spiritual reality we are called to participate in? Based on my understanding, I would say they are both.

> God is love. Whoever lives in love lives in God, and God in them.
>
> 1 John 4:16, NIV

We are invited to live inside the love of Jesus and thus live inside of Him (because love is the essence of who He is). He in turn lives inside us. Here we find our lives agree with heaven and become the places where the great flashes of His tangible glory and presence can be seen and experienced through us as we follow Him.

Lightning strikes are the manifestations of the kingdom of heaven where the sick are healed, the broken restored, the despised cherished, the dead raised, the captives set free, lives and nations changed. We are invited into all of this and more.

The Cloud of Witnesses

> Now it came to pass, about eight days after these sayings, that He took Peter, John, and James and went up on the mountain to pray. As He prayed, the appearance of His face was altered, and His robe became white and glistening. And behold, two men talked with Him, who were Moses and Elijah.
>
> Luke 9:28–30

When I began to meditate on the story of the Transfiguration, I also caught a glimpse of part of the more I believe Father wants to release in this day. Along with the lightnings

222

of heaven, there is another supernatural reality beginning to be poured out in this season. Remember, my friend, everything Jesus walked is fully legal and totally available to us.

Jesus went up into the mountain with His closest friends where He was transfigured. Remember we have said these mountains also speak of high places of government in the spiritual realm? In this place of spiritual encounter, we see Moses and Elijah speaking with Him. Jesus was engaging the cloud of witnesses.

> Therefore we also, since we are surrounded by so great a cloud of witnesses, let us lay aside every weight, and the sin which so easily ensnares us, and let us run with endurance the race that is set before us.
>
> Hebrews 12:1

The cloud of witnesses is very real. If Jesus spoke with them in an encounter, so can we. Some of you might have thought it was strange when I mentioned meeting Enoch in heaven. But meeting and interacting with other people in heaven, as God allows, is quite normal. And sometimes their presence even turns up right here when we engage the unseen realm of God's kingdom like Jesus did on the mountain in Luke 9.

I am sure some of you might find this a bit stretching. I have heard some people express very legitimate concerns that this might be necromancy. I want to assure you it is not. Necromancy is when a person commonly called a medium engages the demonic realm to "speak with the dead." Mediums interact with familiar spirits that take on the image of the person they are conjuring up. This is utterly demonic, and we should have nothing to do with it.

Interacting with the cloud of witnesses, on the occasions that they may turn up in an encounter, is not speaking with the dead, but the living. As we grow in our understanding of how to fully live in the supernatural inheritance that belongs to us in Jesus, happenings such as these may very well become more common.

> But Peter and those with him were heavy with sleep; and when they were fully awake, they saw His glory and the two men who stood with Him. Then it happened, as they were parting from Him, that Peter said to Jesus, "Master, it is good for us to be here; and let us make three tabernacles: one for You, one for Moses, and one for Elijah"—not knowing what he said. While he was saying this, a cloud came and overshadowed them; and they were fearful as they entered the cloud. And a voice came out of the cloud, saying, "This is My beloved Son. Hear Him!"
>
> Luke 9:32–35

I absolutely love Peter's response to what he has experienced. "Jesus, let's just build us a monument of this movement and camp out here on this mountain. Yeah, that's what we should do! Boy, can I get an amen to that?" Peter once again makes me feel so much more normal. How many times have I wanted to stay on the mountain of encounter with God?

I also love that Peter got interrupted by God in mid-speak and was told basically to pipe down and listen to Jesus. How many times has Papa had to interrupt my ideas to tell me the same thing? Thanks, Peter. You make us all feel like we have a chance at living this invitation out.

We are most definitely called to remember times and places of visitation. Like we have said before, the memories of past encounters can become the very context for engaging new ones. But remembering and remaining are two entirely different things.

When Jesus and the disciples descended the mountain, the next story in Luke finds Jesus healing and setting a child tormented by demons free. God fully intends our times of visitation and encounter on the mountain with Him to bring deliverance and freedom to others in the valley.

I contend every day to live in intimacy with Jesus where His kingdom breaks loose all around me. Not where I work harder, but out of the place of rest He is building on the inside of me, where I become a resting place for His presence. In other words, I want to carry the reality I experience on the mountain down into the darkness of the valley.

We are invited, to quote John G. Lake again, into a life "submerged in God, buried up in God, in-filled with God, revealing God." Please, Jesus, make this true of me.

We—you and I—are called to become holy lightning rods for heaven that attract the full power and provision of His kingdom to burst forth in every situation in which we find ourselves. God is not looking for lives that are textbook case studies in the right terminology or strategy; He is looking for lives lived as fiery love stories that ignite nations to burn with the glory of who He is.

So, why not you, my sweet friend? All He is waiting for is for you to say yes with your life. Then all heaven will break loose, hell won't stand a chance, and the Lamb will receive His reward through your life laid down in love. Selah. Let's pause and think on that.

Restoring the Places Long Devastated

> They will rebuild the ancient ruins and restore the places long devastated; they will renew the ruined cities that have been devastated for generations.
>
> Isaiah 61:4, NIV

In chapter 1 when our journey was just beginning together, I shared with you something I once heard Bill Johnson say. He said, "We owe the world an encounter with God." As our journey is drawing to a close, for the purpose of this book at least, I want to return to this statement.

We are called into the place of daily living in encounter with God so that we become His encounter to our world. After all, we cannot give away something we ourselves do not possess. His invitation into the supernatural life is about far more than having a nice experience. We are invited to let our lives become the very places where the people we meet on our journey can experience Him in love and power.

> And if you give yourself to the hungry and satisfy the desire of the afflicted . . . those from among you will rebuild the ancient ruins; you will raise up the age-old foundations; and you will be called the repairer of the breach, the restorer of the streets in which to dwell.
>
> Isaiah 58:10, 12, NASB

What does it look like to be a restorer of places long devastated? What does it look like to become heaven's encounter to the desperation around you?

One afternoon I walked out of the markets in our dusty city of Yei to be introduced to a little girl with burnt orange rags tied on by a plastic bag. I did not know then that she would teach me much about the restoration of God. Her hair matted and eyes wild, she stared and rocked.

"She is deaf," the growing crowd explained. Everyone was curious why the three white women (myself and two of our missionaries) were stopping to inquire about a little beggar girl who couldn't hear. "Her mom and dad are dead. No family. She lives and sleeps on the streets." They said it nonchalantly, like one recounts the latest weather.

She sat fumbling with some knotted string. This little one with special needs, severely abused by men, starving and tormented by the evil around her: Her life was a picture of the devastation Jesus wants to restore.

She was all of maybe eight or nine years old; of course I took her home. Ones like her were the reason I came here five years ago. Some days my staff has been reluctant to let me out of the gate. I always seem to come back with another lost child found.

No one, including her, knew her name. She was nameless. To the world around her, she didn't even exist. Not really. Her birth mama died or abandoned her. Either way the result was the same. She had grown among the rubbish so long she started to blend in with it.

But to the One who created her, she was an absolute treasure. All heaven was waiting for this moment, its breath held as we first met. She took one look at me and called out "*Mama*" in muffled monotone tones. I took her in my arms and whispered, "Yes, my daughter. *Ay, benia tai.*"

Her eyes smiled in response. We named her Mercy as we all piled into the car together, three missionaries and a little girl found, on our way to go for lunch before heading home. In an instant the devastation of her world began to change.

No longer eating rotting trash, she sat with us at a table. Honored. Loved. The waitress helped me wash her hands. Mercy tried to give me her Coke. *No, sweetheart. This is yours. All yours.*

Our hungry little girl ate two helpings of meat and cassava (a root that is beaten and boiled into a sticky porridge). Her language garbled, she gestured erratically, clawing at my arms in pure excitement. I looked into her eyes across the table and saw far more than her looking back at me. I rejoiced knowing we follow the One who still comes to set the captives free.

We got home and our staff gave me their "we can't let you out of our sight" look. How many times already this year had I left home for bread or fabric and come back with a child! And this one was a very special treasure with very special needs. Our resources already stretched beyond reason, I silently stormed heaven for grace on their behalf.

Mercy dug her nails into my arm like a scared animal. She was only acting out the role she had been treated as. What would happen when she would be cherished and treated as the royalty she truly is?

One of my daughters, also rescued from a life lived in back alleys, came up to me, her eyes all shiny. She told me in our local Arabic, "Mama, thank you for bringing her home. All the bad spirits that are tormenting her will go because we will pray, and Jesus will make them go. Then she will be healed." I smiled deep and hugged my gift from heaven. A child led again.

Mercy's coming to stay with us brought with it His invitation to give our lives away. We held her and dodged her swipes, and whispered peace. We commanded darkness to bow, broke the curses and lies and called forth life.

Her first night with us, we tucked her in the first bed she had slept in in at least two years, all snuggled warm with her very own blanket. She laughed. Over and over again she laughed and said His name. Jesus.

By the time freedom began to come, I was a bit bruised and sore from her blows, tuckered out from restraining her attacks and teary-eyed grateful for her transformation, which has been nothing short of, well, supernatural.

This one, we were told, who was deaf and unable to communicate, had only death and fear in her gaze and anger in her grip, has become like a new child. It did not come easily. But restoration has begun.

Thank You, Jesus, for Mercy and grace in times of need. Thank You for the entire reality that what I experience in You, I am privileged to pour out on places and lives long devastated. And in Your amazing love, You come and transform them.

Burning Signposts of Another Realm

My sweet friend, one thing my years in Africa are teaching me: Light has to do only one thing to win. Show up.

Often that is 90 percent of the battle. Showing up. Sometimes people ask me what ministry I am in. I tell them I am in the ministry of showing up. By grace, my goal each day is to show up filled up, ready to be poured out on a hungry and hurting world.

God is asking us—you and me—to be burning signposts of another realm. Signposts are planted in one place to show the way to another place. They are not the destination themselves.

Can you imagine being in Florida, seeing your first sign for Texas and then parking your vehicle at the sign and celebrating having arrived? Would you do that? Of course you wouldn't. So many things God does in and through our lives on this supernatural journey are simply signposts pointing to a reality that is so much greater than we can ask, think or imagine.

God desires our lives—your life and my life—to become burning signposts of His love and grace that make His realm real, right in the messy, muddy here and now. Right in the middle of our everyday world.

> Love has been perfected among us in this: that we may have boldness in the day of judgment; because as He is, so are we in this world.
>
> 1 John 4:17

God is relentlessly committed to making us look like Him. That simple. His love being matured in our lives brings great boldness, even when the world around us shakes. We can be bold, because we are rooted and grounded in His kingdom that cannot be shaken.

Yes, indeed. Even in the deepest darkness, light wins. Truly there is no contest.

And so here we are called to carry His kingdom, the jurisdiction of His light, fearlessly into the night. I have never seen darkness put out light. Instead, the smallest flame causes the greatest darkness to flee before its burning. *Jesus, set me on fire with a flame that burns with who You are and chases away the night with Your brightness.*

All of what we have shared together in these pages is about embracing a journey, not arriving at a destination. A. W.

Tozer says, "Faith is not a conclusion you reach. . . . It's a journey you live." And the most important journeys always start deep inside us. We become what we behold. So let us fix our gazes on the One who is a consuming fire that He might transform us to look like who He is.

We have barely scratched the surface of God's amazing invitations to us. It will take us the rest of time and eternity to explore them all.

But know this. You are invited in. You are not asked to stand on the outside and look in on someone else's journey, someone else's encounter or someone else's story. You have your own amazing adventure with Jesus and His kingdom that awaits you.

You, precious friend, are invited into a relationship with our beautiful, dangerous King who wants to consume you with His blazing grace and overwhelm you with His love. Right here, right now, there is a call to step off the paved road, off the known path, and begin your own journey into His wild, untamed heart.

Does this excite you? Does it scare you? Maybe a little of both? Me too. But an unknown future does not have to be scary if we know the One who holds it.

God is calling out a company of those who are willing to embrace His unknown paths, to stand at the crossroads and see again. He is calling out a company of those who will ask for the ancient ways, the good ways, and walk in them (see Jeremiah 6:16). He is looking for a company who will walk like Enoch: birthed from humility, matured in intimacy, launched out into destiny.

Did some of our time together stretch your comfort zones? It is okay if it did. If we never stretch, we never grow. It is even quite fine if you disagree with parts. We are all in different places on our journeys with Jesus. There is total grace for you to be you and to be right where you are. Just keep seeking, keep knocking, keep asking for the *more* Papa longs to give you.

I hope you have found some keys through our time together to help you on your journey deeper into His heart. As I said in the very beginning, my goal in writing this book has been to simply share my adventure with you as a friend and offer whatever I am learning on it that might be a blessing. Thank you so much for the grace of a shared journey.

Truly, I am honored by your presence here. Thank you for spending your time with these words. This I know. You, incredible you, reading this sentence right now, have an amazing destiny you were created for in Jesus.

It is far bigger than you can imagine. It extends far beyond what your natural eyes see. And it begins simply with your saying yes to His invitation to the supernatural life.

May I pray for you?

Papa, I am so grateful for all the words and pages my friend and I have been privileged to share together. I am humbled by his trust, by her trust to allow me to share so openly, so transparently. Thank You for the grace of shared journeys in You.

I ask as this dear one stands at the crossroads of Your ancient paths that You would make Your ways very clear. I ask, Papa, that this one with an incredible destiny in You, that we might be part of a whole movement of people You are raising up today to live from heaven to earth and bring Your kingdom with love and power. In the fullness of all Jesus is I pray, Amen.

Discussion Questions and Activation Exercise

- What does it mean to you to live a life in agreement with heaven?
- What areas of your life might Jesus want to align for greater agreement that they would become contact points for His lightnings? Talk to Him about each one.
- Have you ever had an encounter with the cloud of witnesses? Ask Papa to teach you about their reality and function.
- What encounters on the mountain with God have you had that you wanted to memorialize with a monument instead of moving with the revelation and reality you received into the valley to bring freedom? When you did move into the valley, how did the reality you experienced on the mountain change the circumstances around you?
- What places long devastated is God calling you to join Him in restoring?
- Have you ever been tempted to park at a sign in the Spirit? What was it and what reality was it pointing toward?
- Ask the Holy Spirit to teach you about the ancient paths in Jeremiah 6:16.

Activation: Make a list of what has impacted you most profoundly from this book. Pick the three things that stand out to you as the most pertinent for your journey right now. Take them to Jesus, and ask Him to show you how to grow in each of these areas with Him.

Take a look at the Enoch Compact in the epilogue. If it expresses your desire, pray it back to God as a commitment before Him, filling in the blanks with what is in your heart. Feel free to put its concepts in your own words and, like everything in our journey together, use it as a stepping-off place for your own adventures on the unpaved road into His heart.

Epilogue

The Enoch Compact

Father, I thank You that You are raising up a company of people who walk like Enoch . . . that You are raising up a company of people who embrace the unknown paths of Your presence, who dance through the storms of our day and who carry the lightnings of heaven to change the world around them.

Right now, I intentionally set my desire to become a part of all that You are doing in the earth in this moment. I fully accept and embrace Your invitation to the supernatural life I am created for.

In Your grace, I choose to step lower in humility before You, deeper into intimacy with You and further out into my destiny in You.

I ask You, Holy Spirit, to teach me about each of these areas. Open my eyes to see, my ears to hear and my heart to receive everything of Your kingdom that You desire to pour into and through my life.

In the fullness of all You are, Jesus, I pray, Amen.

Where God is asking me to step lower in humility before Him:

_____

_____

_____

_____

Where God is calling me to step deeper in intimacy with Him:

_____

_____

_____

_____

Where God is launching me out further into my destiny in Him:

_____

_____

_____

_____

Author-Recommended Resources for Going Deeper:

- Bill Johnson and Bethel Church, Redding, California: www.ibethel.org
- Graham Cooke: On hiddenness and manifestation, and many other things, too. www.grahamcooke.com
- Ian Clayton: He takes some of the areas we have touched on and goes into greater depth with them. He is not for the faint of heart. http://sonofthunder.org.nz/
- Francis and Judith MacNutt: Judith just released a new book about the angelic, and together both are pioneers in the healing ministry. www.christianhealingmin.org
- Randy Clark: Another pioneer in raising up a supernatural company who walks in the love and power of Jesus. www.globalawakening.com
- Martin Scott: A prophetic papa from the UK sharing dialogue and resources on engaging society and social transformation. http://3generations.eu/blog/

Michele Perry is a visionary and creative whirlwind. An artist, author and photographer, she travels roughly a third of her time to speak and share the lessons she is learning on this unpaved road into God's heart. She spends much of her remaining time in the bush of South Sudan without running water or electricity. And her idea of camping is still a day spa. Go figure!

She's simply in love with Jesus. Her favorite places are trash heaps and unreached villages . . . and the occasional day spa.

Michele longs to see a supernatural company of people who take walking lessons from Enoch be released to soar into the wildest dreams of God, embrace the audacity of heaven and live in two realms at once.

Michele's first book was *Love Has a Face*. She is the founding National Field Coordinator for Iris Ministries, Inc., in South Sudan and is ordained by Heidi and Rolland Baker under Iris Ministries. Michele is also the founder/director of Nema International, Inc. She writes regularly at http://fromtheunpavedroad.com and is frequently available for speaking engagements in the West.

Michele also writes for The Enoch Company. Her periodic articles and insights on deeper living in God and embracing the supernatural life can be found at http://enochco.com.